James Sayles Brown

Partisan politics, the evil and the remedy

an analysis of the great political parties of the country

James Sayles Brown

Partisan politics, the evil and the remedy
an analysis of the great political parties of the country

ISBN/EAN: 9783743438200

Printed in Europe, USA, Canada, Australia, Japan

Cover: Foto ©Suzi / pixelio.de

More available books at **www.hansebooks.com**

PARTISAN POLITICS

THE EVIL AND THE REMEDY

AN ANALYSIS OF THE GREAT POLITICAL PARTIES OF THE
COUNTRY—THEIR MORALS AND METHODS—AS
THE SUPREME POWER IN THE REPUBLIC

THE REMEDY PROHIBITIVE LEGISLATION

BY

JAMES SAYLES BROWN

LOS ANGELES, CAL.

" Then none was for a party ;
Then all were for the State ;
Then the great men helped the poor,
And the poor man loved the great ;
The lands were fairly portioned ;
Then spoils were fairly sold ;
The Romans were like brothers
In the brave days of old."

MACAULEY—*Lays of Ancient Rome*

PHILADELPHIA
PRINTED BY J. B. LIPPINCOTT COMPANY
1897

PRICE, 50 CENTS

CONTENTS.

CHAPTER XXI.

CHAPTER XXII.

CHAPTER XXIII.

PARTISAN POLITICS.

CHAPTER I.

PROLOGUE. THE GENESIS OF PARTIES.

These pages will be devoted to the discussion of the following proposition: Those organizations known as political parties, through whose exclusive agency all the powers and functions of the governments, State and national, are exercised and controlled, each claiming to be, *par excellence*, the representatives and servants of the people, and to be laboring earnestly and unselfishly in promoting the common welfare, are, in fact, combinations and minorities of the voting population who have conspired to seize and hold the government, with all its institutions, powers, offices, and emoluments, and use them primarily and exclusively in the interests of the party and its favorites. Though the purposes of these formidable and rival political factions are well understood, and are sanctioned and encouraged by the great majority of the electors, they are, nevertheless, hostile to free institutions and the liberties of the people, and as such should be subjected to the restraints and prohibitions of law.

A reform in politics of the radical nature here suggested will strike the average voter who is strongly

attached to his party as a proposal altogether extravagant and impracticable, if not utterly absurd in conception.   With the great mass of the voting population of this country the political sentiment which
binds them to the party organizations is as strong and
enduring as the religious sentiment cherished among
Christians of the various sects, and it is not improbable
that there are more backsliders among the Christian
converts than are found among the adherents of the
great parties.   Nevertheless, there is left to us a large
number of thoughtful and earnest citizens who cherish our free institutions, with the love which the
fathers manifested for them, who see in the decay of
public morals the degeneracy of our representative
men, and in the increasing power of the political combinations which already rule and despoil us one of the
greatest perils of the republic.

With a fraction of these citizens we hope amicably
to discuss this subject.   We write for them, for with
right-minded minorities all genuine reforms must begin.

The writer, for more than twenty years of his life,
was an active partisan in the political field, and during
that period the incumbent of several offices.   Until
his recent acquisition of citizenship in the State of
California he had been for thirty years a continued
resident of the District of Columbia.   For many years
he has not cast a vote with any party organization,
and has no party prejudices or preferences.   He has
had much observation and some experience of the
political methods in vogue throughout the country,

and hopes, therefore, to be able to treat the subject in hand intelligibly and without prejudice or passion.

The rise of political parties in this country dates back to about the year 1787. Previous to that time the methods now in use in the management and control of such organizations were comparatively unknown. In that year a constitutional convention assembled in Philadelphia to establish a national constitution for the government of the country. In the debates on the drafting of the instrument marked differences of opinion were soon developed, which resulted practically in dividing the body into two opposing parties. This tendency appeared in a form quite as decided and irreconcilable in the State conventions to which the instrument was submitted for acceptance. These differences of opinion consisted, on the one hand, in a tendency to maintain freedom of action for the individual citizen, and for the several States independence in legislation and administration, and in everything, indeed, except the foreign policy and the national defences of the Union. On the other hand, the tendency was to subordinate the States to the national authority and clothe it with powers commensurate with its responsibility and dignity as the ruling power of the nation.

The advocates of a central national authority soon became known as Federalists. The opposite party took the name of Republicans, or Democrats, or Democrat-Republicans, Thomas Jefferson leading the latter, and Alexander Hamilton the former of these then recognized divisions of the political sentiment of the country. These new parties, though they did not possess the advantages of organization and the means of support which are so readily obtainable at the present day, nevertheless grew apace and shared the public confidence. They had their separate candidates for the Presidency and for the different State offices, and their party leaders in the Senate and House of Representatives.

The Federalists were in power under the administration of Washington and Adams until the year 1800, when the Republicans succeeded them, with Jefferson as President, who held the office for eight years. He was followed by Mr. Madison and Mr. Monroe, who each were in office for eight years. This period from 1788 to 1824 may be said to be the formative period in the development of party organization in American politics.

Other issues began to arise between these parties of a commercial, economic, and diplomatic nature. There was much party bitterness, and malice even, manifested in the literature and discussions of the partisans of the day; a wholesale detraction of their opponents and a general disregard for truth and common courtesy were the chief vices of the politicians of that period; but there was comparatively little of that tendency, afterwards exhibited in so many forms, to make merchandise of the powers and resources of the State and of the rights of individual citizens.

Sectional divisions soon arose among the leading politicians who joined in electing Mr. Monroe in 1820, and under the influence of the personal hostility existing between Henry Clay and Andrew Jackson two great parties again appeared upon the stage in about the year 1830. One of these organizations, under the name of Democrats, supported the doctrines and public measures of the Jeffersonian Republicans. The other section took the name of the National Republican, and finally the Whig party. They represented many of the views and traditions of the Federalists. These two organizations, which contended with one another with varied success for over thirty years, were succeeded by the present Democratic and Republican parties.

The tenure of office under the earlier Presidents was practically for life, or during good behavior. Appointments were made on the merits of the appointee, and public office was regarded as a trust of much responsibility, as well as honor. Washington in eight years removed only nine persons. John Adams removed the same number in four years. Jefferson in eight years removed thirty-nine persons; and in the twenty years following there were but sixteen removals from office. In fact, from April 30, 1789, to March 4, 1829, there were but seventy-four removals from office, and out of this number, five were defaulters to the government. But between March 4, 1829, and March 22, 1830, the number of changes made in the civil service amounted to about two thousand.

General Jackson on his accession to the Presidency announced in his message rotation in office as Democratic doctrine. In the practical application of this rule of his administration he removed five hundred postmasters during the first year of his executive rule. Senator Marcy, of New York, a Democratic leader in the Senate in 1832, in a speech in defence of partisan removals and short terms of office, said, "They," meaning the New York politicians, "when contending for victory, avow the intention of enjoying the fruits of it. They see nothing wrong in the rule that 'to the victor belong the spoils' of the enemy." This doctrine had been pretty well exemplified and permanently established by the action of the Democratic party of the Empire State. It is generally conceded, perhaps, by everybody outside of that party that the spoils system was inaugurated and had its first party recognition under the administration of General Jackson. Its rivals were not slow in adopting the same policy and like measures in securing its success. The spoils system had at this period been adopted and was flourishing with ominous success in the local politics of both New York and Pennsylvania. It was perhaps inevitable that it should be introduced into national politics.

The increasing wealth and population of the country and the rapidity with which new civil communities were springing up all over the land increased the activity of the politicians and opened a wide-spread and inviting field to the demagogue and the soldier of fortune in political warfare. This condition of things was in a large measure due to some unfortunate legislation obtained about this time for party purposes. In 1820, Mr. Crawford, a distinguished Democrat from a Southern State, procured the passage of a law limiting the tenure of office to four years. This unwise and dangerous provision of law was advocated on the ground of justice to that large class of citizens who desired to share in the honors and responsibilities of public office. It was urged that such a law would have a tendency to equalize the honors and emoluments of office among the people, and prevent the politicians and placemen from monopolizing these desirable positions and holding them indefinitely. This measure was generally accepted at the time of its enactment as a popular stroke of legislation and a scheme adapted to give to a larger number of citizens a share in the immediate administration of public affairs, and thus increase the numbers of those who would have an intelligent and direct interest in the execution of the laws and promoting in a multitude of ways the general welfare. Time has shown that it was really one of the most mischievous and dangerous acts that was ever passed by the American Congress. It was really a party device to increase the amount of patronage available for party purposes. Its immediate effect was to increase enormously the patronage of the government and multiply the numbers and encourage the hopes of the many who were engaged in the scramble for office. It exerted a wide-spread influence in demoralizing the civil service and in diminishing its general efficiency.

Thus at an early day after the adoption of the Constitution did these organizations obtain an ascendency in American politics which has been constantly growing more assured and more tyrannical and corrupt as the nation has advanced in civilization and material progress.

CHAPTER II.

SECTARIAN POLITICS.

Our first accusation against the parties who divide the political sentiment of the country to-day is that they are clannish, selfish, and exclusive in a marked degree. A simple statement of the real purpose and business of these organizations, the chief end and aim which inspires all their zeal and compensates them for all their labor, is sufficient to impeach them as unworthy the confidence of a free people, and prompt the earnest inquiry from every impartial citizen, Why are they permitted to exist? If they were free associations admitting to their fellowship citizens of every shade of political opinion, if they were controlled by the wisest and best men of the nation even, they would be dangerous to the liberties of the people; and as organizations established outside and independent of the government for the purpose of controlling its action and wielding its authority, whatever may be their character otherwise, they would be unworthy of the support of honest men. But they have not this plea even of good intentions and patriotic motives in their behalf. They assume to be discharging the functions of government which they have usurped, for the sole benefit of their fellow-citizens at large, while, in fact, such organizations are primarily maintained for the exclusive benefit of those who actively sustain it. It is a conspiracy, often openly avowed, on the part of certain combinations of citizens to seize the offices, honors, and emoluments which pertain to the government service, and distribute them exclusively among the members of the successful party. Democrats cannot share in any of these honors and responsibilities while Republicans are in power. A Republican who sets up any claim to share the benefits of a Democratic victory in an election will only excite the derision and contempt of all parties. They are simply political joint stock and mutual benefit associations, conducted solely in the interests of their membership. Its partisan adherents and followers may be divided into two classes: first, those who have talent, influence, or position, or can control a large voting constituency; second, the rank and file of the organization who do the voting, the shouting, and the booming which constitutes so important a part in the election of candidates for office. The first class, who are the leaders and directors of the combination, find their compensation for their labors in the possession of the offices, perquisites, and honors captured by the party. As the lions of the organization they take by common consent the lion's share of whatever the association captures under the rules of political warfare. The second and larger class of citizens look for their compensation in such legisla-

tion as will favor their interests or improve their business, or that of the class or guild to which they belong. They have a pride, furthermore, in being members of a large and powerful association patronized and championed by a host of distinguished men.

Everybody knows, or, at least, has the evidence to believe, that these are the sole considerations that keep these organizations in existence, and that without them it would be impossible to sustain a political party as a permanent organization in any State in the Union. How often in the strifes of these partisans do we hear it said, and the party press of both sides declare, of the rival party, that it is kept together only by the cohesive power of public plunder. These jobbing conspirators believe what they aver, and from evidence of which they are excellent judges; and, what is more, every intelligent citizen holds the same opinion. If there were no spoils to be obtained, men enough could not be found to maintain these cumbrous organizations and do so vast an amount of work at such sacrifice of time and money simply for the purpose of instructing the masses as to their duties as members of the body politic.

Thus it may be confidently averred of these parties that the prime object of their existence, and of all their zeal and labor in the political field, is to secure place and the emoluments of power under government patronage and protection. Their loud professions of superior intelligence, virtue, and patriotism, like the stale multiloquence of the showman and the mountebank, is a mere device to inspire confidence and allay honest suspicion in the minds of the masses to whose ears they mostly address themselves. There is nothing new to us in this general condition of a voluntary association, ostensibly formed for wise and good purposes and in the interest of the public. Such organizations are multiplied on every hand, some of them of a religious and benevolent order, originally instituted by wise men, which at length, falling into the hands of ambitious and mercenary combinations, become agencies of corruption, oppression, and crime.

There are many people in these great political associations of superior merits as citizens, and as Christians even, but they can do little or nothing towards changing the chief purposes of their action, their methods, or their general character. They are the mere servants and followers of those who lead and govern the great coalition. Upright and conscientious men are not eligible even, under the party allotment, to the offices of inferior grades. The great body of the electors of the country who have given their fealty and support to these parties are silent partners in the joint concern, and have little influence, and so naturally feel but slight responsibility in regard to their general management. A spartan phalanx of placemen, bred and skilled in the tactics of political promotion, have obtained possession of all the forces and machinery of these organizations, and use them as a stock company uses a mine or a mill, to produce for its shareholders the largest

2

possible dividends. The earnings and honors of the association can be shared only by those who are members of it. The Democratic party is for Democrats and for none others; all it achieves and acquires is for Democrats only. The same is true of the Republican party in every particular. While either of these, or any other similar organization, is in the ascendency, it is well understood that, as a rule, nobody outside of them will be permitted to hold places of honor and trust under the government, or share in the peculiar advantages which come to the party which wins a Presidential election. The chief burden of the executive office and the principal business of the heads of departments is to furnish places for the members of their own party after its accession to power. If these gentlemen do not use extraordinary diligence and skill in turning out their political opponents and in making vacancies for the benefit of their own political brotherhood, they will subject themselves to the severest criticism by the party throughout the country. That official who would appoint a member of a rival organization to any salaried position, or a non-partisan citizen to any public office, or who would favor any such general policy, would be denounced as a traitor to the party, and would soon lose his political standing, if not his official head. If they can prevent it, no one outside of their ranks will be permitted to hold any place of honor or profit, or be in any position as a representative of the people. Thus they maintain an unyielding monopoly of all these high privileges and sacred trusts which pertain to the government of a free people. They manifest such a degree of intolerance in proscribing all who are not members of their conclave, that one is led to fear that they might, under the pressure of great competition, disfranchise all persons who do not prove their allegiance to it. To gerrymander the enemy's district, to illegally challenge or destroy his vote, to count him out, or contest his seat after he is legally elected, are common devices practised by rival political organizations, and grave bodies like State Legislatures and the national Congress will aid and abet in these crimes against human liberties.

Such being the character of these combinations, selfish and clannish, ambitious of power and doubtful honors, with almost unlimited access to the public treasury, who need be surprised that they are unscrupulous and corrupt in their methods, debauching the public service and all persons connected with it? What else are they likely to be than a disturbing and dangerous force in the body politic and a constant menace to the integrity of our representative system of government and our free institutions? Who does not know that they lower the standard of public morals and deprave the sentiments of patriotism and honor which the American people have been so long taught sacredly to cherish?

CHAPTER III.

THEIR TENDENCY TO DEGRADE THE CIVIL SERVICE.

WITH such parties, selfish, ambitious, and exclusive, in possession of the government, what kind of a
civil service might we naturally expect them to
maintain under our free suffrage and unrestricted
immigration into the country? Would they not un-
questionably degrade it to a very low standard of
qualification and efficiency? Would it not be thoroughly partisan, incompetent, and corrupt? From
the composition and general character of all political
organizations in this country, they are quite unfitted
for the responsibilities they assume and the duties
they are called upon to discharge. Anybody can be
a Republican, or a Democrat, or a Populist in politics. We are all eligible to membership in these associations, without respect to race, condition, color,
antecedents, or moral character. No man who has a
vote will be blackballed or denied party fellowship
by reason of unfortunate idiosyncrasies or disabilities, mental or moral. All the people want to vote,
and each man chooses a partisan organization
through which he hopes to make his vote and his
political endeavors effective. A very large share of
these citizens would like something in the way of
honors or perquisites, as a result of their labors in
this connection. Though they are too modest to take
openly the position of candidates for office, they have

secret hopes and aspirations that they may be favorably considered in the party allotment of places. Others, and they are not a few in numbers, are very anxious to hold office of almost any grade, or in some other way serve the public for a stipulated consideration. Hence each party is composed of a very miscellaneous company of voting citizens who are desirous of serving their country in a position of honor and profit./ The drummers and recruiting sergeants of these organizations are generally demagogues who have expectations in the increase of the party vote, and they want therefore, votes in any possible number and in any way they can be obtained. They therefore, as they say, appeal to the masses and hold meetings where the common people can be most easily reached. They make special appeals to the poor man, the man out of a job, and the man who wants a change or a rotation in office, to the citizens of foreign birth, to the idle and vicious, and promise them immunity from the ills of life, and general prosperity, if they come into the party fold. From this muster of partisan forces, which constitute a numerical majority of every popular organization, are selected the persons who are to occupy places of trust and power in the service of the public; or rather from the ranks of the dominant party only will these selections be made, for they will hold a monopoly of this distribution. This appointment of the prizes won in battle from the enemy will be made in strict accordance with the doctrine of rewards and punishments,—punishing your enemies by turning them out of office, and rewarding your friends by putting them in the vacant positions you make.

In the history of party organizations it will be found that they generally arise out of some public want and consequent demand; some needed reform is imperative, some important changes are required in the financial, commercial, or economic conditions of the country. The inauguration of a new party in politics is always an experiment. Such enter-prizes offer little to corrupt even ambitious men, who have nothing to risk for the public good merely, so that the burden of initiating and launching a new movement of this character upon an uncertain sea is generally taken up by a class of earnest, pub-lic-spirited, and more or less conscientious citizens. They are a class generally who have no axes to grind, and who are laboring generously, if not solely, for the public good. Now this party while it is young and vigorous, having little experience in public affairs, and but little discipline in party tac-tics, will be comparatively a pure and patriotic asso-ciation; but when it has once partaken of the honors that pertain to official place it is sure to de-velop that lust for spoils which is innate in the car-nal mind that has a turn for politics. As soon as it has a pay-roll and a cash-box,—in other words, as soon as it can create vacancies in official positions and fill them at will,—as sure as it can get posses-sion and control of the United States treasury it will be sure of a large accession from the older party organizations. That numerous class of mercenaries who follow and feed upon the spoils of the victors, the broken politicians, the bosses out of a job, together with the great body who constitute the floating vote, will go over to the new party, with the instinct of gentler animals who are always seeking fresh feeding-grounds. This is a general history of all the political parties that have ever existed in this country. As an Irishman would say, they never can be trusted with power except when they are in the minority.

Now, from these political unions there must be chosen the persons to whom we intrust the entire administration of government, State and national, involving the liberties, the property, and the lives of the people. There are good men enough, intelligent, honest, and capable, to fill these official places with credit to themselves and the country, but the party rule by which they are distributed is such, and the standard of qualification for holding the highest offices even is so low and depraved, that citizens of the better class have little chance of being elected for these responsible trusts, or of remaining long in them if they should fortunately be chosen. These partisan associations are of a popular character, composed ostensibly of compatriots and sympathizers, and they keep open house every day in the year. Entire political equality, the sentiment that one man is as good as another, that there is no official position that the meanest man may not aspire to and attain by any of the methods sanctioned by party usage, are cardinal doctrines in American politics. Taking advantage of the growing sentiment in the country for liberty, equality, and fraternity, the grosser elements of these organizations inevitably assert themselves and claim the high privileges of their citizenship and their party allegiance. The ambitious, the mercenary and venal among them, the bold, bad men of every caste, become active in the competitive struggle for place or some remunerative service under the government. By sheer physical exertion and endurance, by shouldering and bullying, by acts of violence and fraud, they soon create an atmosphere around them in which an honest man cannot live, and in which no self-respecting gentleman will wish long to remain. These worthy citizens generally retire in disgust from any active service, and leave a clear field to those who are less fastidious as to their associates and are not thin-skinned and squeamish about the tactics to be employed in political warfare. This unscrupulous class of partisans are insatiate and persistent in their hunger for office; they will plot for it and fight for it, and often they will stain their hands with blood to secure it for themselves or their patrons. These methods are quite effective, and those who employ them generally win. This style of men in various guises abound in the political arena, and they multiply rapidly as a party grows older and its revenues and sinecures increase. Such a sphere of action is congenial to, the tastes of a large class of citizens, and it is quite adapted to their peculiar occupations and talents.

It is true, furthermore, that this class of persons have become a necessity of the modern party organizations, especially as they are conducted in the great cities of the country; indeed, no political party can do without them. They require a great variety of service. There is, as is sometimes said, much dirty work to be done; and not unfrequently bloody work is to be done; the bulldozing and shotgun policy of the South, by which the negro vote has been suppressed for the last twenty-five years, is not the only record of violence and bloodshed which the political partisans have furnished for the future historian of the republic. In the great municipalities, where the industrial classes are massed and can be more conveniently manipulated, they are made a factor of no inconsiderable consequence. The slums of the great towns must be worked, and the rural districts canvassed to their remotest corners; false and libellous reports are to be printed and circulated against the candidates of the opposing party; votes are to be purchased; men of foreign birth not entitled to vote are to be registered and kept under surveillance until the day of election; men must be employed to "vote early and vote often through the day;" ballot-boxes are to be stuffed or rifled of their contents; there must be members of the party who can carry clubs and pistols on election day, and use them, too, if the opposing party becomes violent in its conduct at any polling place. Those who have influence with all that class who prey upon society, and whose votes for various considerations are on the market, must be fellowshipped and employed. The saloon

will be the appropriate place of rendezvous and intrigue, and the men who sell intoxicating drinks,
and those who keep disreputable places of resort,
must be chief counsellors as well as purveyors of
the party. These persons can command many votes,
and they will resort to expedients and violate law to
an extent that respectable citizens cannot be induced
to undertake. Their valuable services must, therefore, be retained, and they must be fellowshipped as
fellow-workers in a comon cause.

Now, it is said, in extenuation of these practices
and the employment of these agencies, that all these
things must be done, and supplemented by a multitude of other offences against society and individuals, because the opposing party will resort to the
same methods; and the party organization which
attempts to conduct an honest campaign is sure to
be defeated at the polls. Men trained to this work
must be had; the party who has a monopoly of their
services carries the country and will hold it as long
as party combinations are tolerated and recognized
as agents of the people. This bad element will not
consent to be tolerated simply, but they will require
recognition as fellow-citizens and useful members of
the party. Their methods must be sanctioned and
defended by the rank and file of their colleagues.
These agents and coworkers, furthermore, must be
well paid for such onerous and dangerous services.
They claim to have done all the hazardous and dirty
work of the campaign, and to have really won the
local victories where they reside; they therefore

loudly and persistently demand that their services be suitably recognized and compensated, on the ground that "the laborer is worthy of his hire." They must be paid in patronage and perquisites, the products of their labors; they must have a share of the offices of trust and power which they have aided the party to wrest from the enemy. As they have the means generally of enforcing their claims, they will have preference generally over their collaborators who have done cleaner and less doubtful work. These persons, when they are placed in responsible positions as a reward of their prowess on the field of political strife, spread the contagion of their baneful example throughout the public service. They are pointed out as successful politicians, enjoying the spoils of victory which they have aided the party in securing. Their crimes are condoned by the party and overlooked and apologized for by its most respectable members. A large class of corrupt and unscrupulous men are found eager to equal or excel them as political aspirants.

One of the worst features of the present party methods is the degrading influence of these practices upon the public conscience. Who can doubt that they tend to corrupt the public morals and foster the common vices of society? It would seem that it need not require the discrimination of a Christian minister or the nice perception of a moralist to comprehend the effect of such a public policy on the moral sensibility of a Christian people.

Now, if such is the miscellaneous character and

make-up of these political fraternities; if the rights,
the persons, and services, of all classes are alike to be
respected and rewarded, you will necessarily have a
low standard of qualification for office and a rule of
distribution of prizes that will give successful party
service priority over moral worth, as well as capacity
and experience in public duties. In justice to all the
members of this joint concern, your standard of qualification for office must be adjusted to the capacity,
social standing, and moral worth of the average members of the league. This is true democracy, but a
kind of democracy that crowds the public service with
mediocre men in talents and morals. Hence a man's
general character is not called in question or taken
into consideration at all by the ethics of the great
parties when he is a candidate for office. If he is a
convicted thief, a defaulter, or in other respects
grossly immoral or incompetent, his election or appointment to office may be a doubtful question, though
it by no means may be impossible if he can command
the local strength of his party, or the indorsement of
the party press of his general character with a persistent denial of all the charges made against him. That
a representative in Congress, or a United States senator, or a candidate for the office of President even, is
a man whose social habits should debar him from good
society, a man you would not trust with your money
or the custody of your wife or daughter, will not defeat him for a party nomination or election. Such
men have little chance of political preferment in an
election by the people, except where party machinery

and party discipline have a controlling influence; but a dominant party is generally strong enough to ignore the question of character and general capacity, and place such men in office as the interests of the organization may require. Persons of superior qualifications, who have not attained a standing of influence in the party by a long and distinguished service in its behalf, will have no chance whatever of occupying one of the places of honor and trust.

Under such a rule of distribution of the spoils of office, is it surprising that so many incompetent and corrupt men are everywhere found in public life? that we have pugilists and bullies, drunkards and duelists, and men who have been convicted of various crimes, holding seats as honorable senators and representatives in the national Congress,—men who are denied social recognition at the capitol of the nation? There being no standard of merit except valuable service or political influence, there is seldom any due discrimination exercised by the people or the appointing power in the assignment of places. Hence you will see small men in large places, and large men in small places; as is said, round pegs in square holes, and square pegs in round holes; and not always the right man in the right place, according to business methods. This is abundantly and strikingly illustrated in the departments at Washington. Of the thousands who occupy positions there under the government, every man and woman of them, from cabinet officers to the day laborers and watchmen upon the public buildings and grounds, have obtained their places solely

through the party influence and assistance they have
been able to command.

I am not to be understood as affirming or insin-
uating that all the persons, or a majority of them
even, connected with the civil service of the country
are, as a general rule, either incompetent or immoral
persons.   I am criticising and condemning, rather,
the vicious system in vogue, under which persons are
selected to office under partisan rule.   In regard to
those persons who occupy positions in the depart-
mental service at Washington, I am free to testify,
from an extended acquaintance with a large number
of them, that these departments contain a large body
of able and experienced men and women, who for
general intelligence and moral worth are not excelled
by the inhabitants of any community in the country.
Some of them have been long in the public service,
and are qualified to fill almost any office in the gift of
the people.   Some of them have been members of
Congress, of State Legislatures, judges of courts, literary and professional men.   Some have obtained distinction in the army and the navy and in different
branches of the civil service.   These persons, many of
them, are holding inferior clerkships and working at
low salaries, and with all their vigilance and that of
their friends in resisting the various intrigues by
which the ins go out and the outs go in at the national
capitol, they are gradually being displaced by a class
of political favorites who have neither the experience
nor the general capacity that should qualify them to
fill the vacancies they seek to create.   Each man's

position has depended upon the party influence available to him at the time of his appointment; of this a record is kept by his superiors, and when such influence has lost its potency, unless he has acquired that of a new patron, his tenure of office is very uncertain.

Hence, under this anomalous system of placing persons in responsible positions without a careful consideration of their respective merits, it is not uncommon to find persons in office who are wholly unfitted for the discharge of the duties required of them. You will find a man perhaps sitting as a State legislator who is not a citizen of average intelligence, who is utterly without experience or requisite knowledge of the affairs of his State. He may be the butt of ridicule, even, of his political associates, and have only capacity sufficient to make of himself a most subservient party tool. Another may be a second-rate lawyer who is a third-rate statesman, and is occupying a cabinet position. Or there may be a Secretary of the United States Treasury, who has to deal with the gravest questions of finance, revenue, and commerce, without either acquirements or experience in this varied and responsible service. He is a good stump orator and a thorough-paced politician; his party in his State demanded his appointment, and after immense labor through a series of months he succeeded in obtaining it. If he has the good sense and courage to accept the tutelage of his subordinates in office, and is not ambitious of distinction as lord of the treasury, he may leave a respectable record behind him on retiring from the office; but his party has promised the people a reform in the finances of the country, and he must act promptly and decisively to meet the expectations of the public. Acting under this blind impulse, he becomes a bull in a china-shop.

Now, it is not always true that either the electors or the appointing power of the government are directly responsible for these misfits of the civil service. They are so entirely controlled often by the necessities and dictation of partisan interests that President and cabinet officers, even, must yield their preferences and judgments to the mastery of the chiefs and bosses of the locality most concerned. These high functionaries often complain that they are compelled by these considerations to place men in office who are unfitted to discharge its duties.

It is thus that the public service is degraded and its efficiency greatly impaired. Instead of its being constituted of men and women selected upon a high standard of qualification, persons who are fitted by education and training for the special duties they are to perform, we have a muster of miscellaneous citizens from every occupation and sphere in life. Thousands of these persons, from the want of enterprise and industrious habits, have been unable to obtain in other employments a comfortable support, and have become practically pensioners upon the patronage of the government, rendering it a perfunctory and inadequate service for the salaries paid them. These partisan appointees may by a system of coaching and dry nursing have passed a required civil service examination, but they are poorly fitted to enter as apprentices even into the public service. If in time they acquire sufficient skill in their routine of duties, so as to render them useful and almost necessary to the service, they are liable at any time, by the partisan enforcement of the doctrine of rotation in office, to be displaced by new recruits, who will have to go through the same matriculation and run the same risk of being in their turn discharged by the appointing power.

Now, it need not be urged that these are not business methods, and that no private enterprise could be conducted successfully on such principles. No intelligent citizen could be induced to take stock in any corporation or enter any partnership where the managers or officers of the concern were conducting the business manifestly for their own private advantage, and where its employees were selected from among the friends and relatives solely of the stockholders, with little reference to their general character or their skill and efficiency in the duties assigned them. It is said that the officers and directors of corporations sometimes enter into conspiracies similar to those of the partisans in politics, by which they absorb the profits and exhaust the capital of the concern for the sole benefit of themselves and their co-conspirators. Such persons are called wreckers, in common parlance, because they soon bring such an estate to a condition of insolvency. In such a complot for such objects, both the individuals and the associations engaged in it will naturally degenerate and become more bold, unscrupulous, and criminal in their methods.

This is history. Our politics are growing more

3

turbulent and corrupt, and their influence on our
social condition more pronounced and disastrous.
Where a commonwealth is thus besieged and plun-
dered, its tendency is to drift into lawlessness and
revolution, until its liberties are lost and it becomes
the prey of some ambitious or despotic power. And
yet the generous people of this country will cheerfully
pay the necessary taxes to nurse and support this nefarious and wasteful system, as something due to
patriotism and the country's welfare.

Now, how are you going to eliminate this element
from the political combination? How are you going
to keep these corrupt and dangerous men out of the
parties? Will they go out on mere invitation to do
so? Will a good deal of persistent moral suasion
even induce them either to abandon the sphere of
politics or to act in that sphere as patriots and honest
men? You might as well expect the gamblers and
liquor-sellers of the country to shut their doors
against their customers at the request of the reformers of the day. So long as the civil service is open
to the competition of parties, you may expect that
this class of which we are speaking will be chief
competitors for as well as winners of the prizes so
liberally offered them by the public. So long as rich
prizes can be captured on the high seas without endangering the loss of life or limb, so long will there
be pirates to engage in the destruction of commerce
while it lasts. It is the natural tendency of these
political organizations to draw venal and corrupt
men together for a common purpose. If the ten-

dency in such a combination is to corrupt the better part of its membership as well, how can you have anything as its product but a body of men more or less from their associations unfit for the public service? It is a notorious fact that the moral standard of any association is lower, that it has less moral sensibility, than is conceded to the average of its members. With such a membership as the great parties contain at present, how can we expect anything but a corrupt and wasteful administration of the affairs of the nation? Ye cannot "gather grapes of thorns, or figs of thistles." You can't get good deeds out of bad men, or capacity or honesty out of a political party.

CHAPTER IV.

POLITICAL HERESY.

A PARTY so thoroughly selfish, exclusive, and mercenary will naturally be intensely partisan, and will be intolerant of all opposition to its acts or its opinions. Who is more certain of his position or more dogmatical and intolerant in maintaining the doctrines and usages of his communion than the partisan politician? He has little respect for the man who does not belong to some political party, and he will very industriously attempt to prove to you that every vote cast for a party which is in the minority, or for a person who is not the candidate of some political organization, is a vote lost or thrown away. As though all the votes cast for an unsuccessful candidate of any party were not thrown away. Allegiance to one's party is a well-defined and cherished sentiment with the average citizen everywhere, and is regarded as obligatory as allegiance to the government under which we live, or to the religious sect to which one belongs. It is about as much as a man's reputation is worth to change his political opinions and cease to act with an organization he has once been connected with. Political heresy is as great an offence, in the estimation of a partisan, as is religious heresy in the estimation of the church; the former will be dealt with quite as severely, and be regarded with quite as much distrust, if not contempt, as will the other.

The practice of reading turncoats and dissenters out of the party is quite as common as excommunicating church members for heresy, and is quite as damaging to their general standing in the community and their future prospects in life. He is not only disfellowshipped by his quondam political associates, but they put the beagles of the party press upon his track and run him to cover and disgrace as soon as possible. We complain of the bigotry and intolerance manifested at times by the religious sects, and fail to protest that the political parties are vying with them in the display of these partisan virtues. A religious bigot is one who is blindly devoted to his sect and his creed, whatever errors of doctrine they may uphold, or defects of moral character they apologize for or defend. Intolerance in religion is a desire to suppress all thought and discussion on religious subjects which controvert the religious belief of some sect or individual. This depravity of mind and heart often takes the form of persecution. Tried by these tests the ecclesiastical and political sects will be found about equally illiberal and unfriendly towards those who dissent from their opinions or secede from their order or join a rival organization.

The political parties of the country are notoriously intolerant of any innovation upon the established doctrines and usages of their associations, and will persecute with almost fanatical zeal the man who dares to think or vote adversely to the party platform, or desert into the camp of the enemy. It is a sort of constructive treason against the confederation, which they feel bound to punish conspicuously. This spirit of intolerance was signally illustrated in the treatment which certain distinguished party recreants received at the hands of their former associates during the Presidential campaign of 1896.

The social instinct and the sentiment of loyalty to one's sect or party, guild or clan, is exceedingly strong in the human race. Men love and serve their political parties and their churches with a zeal and devotion very nearly equal in measure ; consequently the great majority of political partisans are of what is termed the thick and thin type; they believe and act with their party right or wrong. They are like well-disciplined soldiers who obey implicitly

the orders of their superiors without questioning the
expediency or justice of such commands. [Many of
the partisans will on occasion boast that they never
have changed and never will change their political
opinions; they vauntingly declare that they are
dyed in the wool Democrats or Republicans, as the
case may be. They are, indeed, born partisans, as
they claim to be. Their endowments and acquirements, mental and moral, fit them to do service as
veterans in the political camp. / They are, as a rule,
bigoted and intolerant, exceedingly conservative and
blind to all corrupt party methods. If they move at
all in the grand column of human progress,—as
move they must,—their evolution is scarcely percep-
tible from year to year. All this is necessary to
make an efficient partisan soldier. You must degrade him to a certain low standard of morals and
intelligence in order to make a subservient party tool
of him as the service requires; as we used to say of
slavery, that you must rob its victim of his manhood
before you could make of him a docile and money-
earning chattel.

No party can maintain the necessary discipline in
a body whose methods are unscrupulous and corrupt,
and whose object is the spoliation of the commonwealth, nor have any general success without a large
body of men of this character in its ranks. In order
to make themselves in the highest degree useful
they must occupy large and commanding space in
the organization. This they are quite apt to claim
on the ground of their devotion to party interests.

Sometimes it happens that a party takes the unpopular side of a public question, or, by reason of a series of political mistakes, legislative, executive, or tactical, it loses the confidence of the public and is repudiated apparently forever by the people. A series of popular elections running through a course of years may give credit to these predictions that it cannot survive its defeats and such a general loss of public confidence. But the old guard of invincibles or unconvincibles are incredulous and hopeful, and remain firm in the support of the organization, as they would do under any conditions of censure or defeat.

This loyalty to party name and party interests, which was strong enough to revoke and annul the loyalty of citizens of the Northern States to the Union and the government which protects and serves us at home and abroad, was signally illustrated in the course of the great majority of the Democratic party during the Southern Rebellion. It is astonishing how many intelligent and Christian men and women in the North sustained to the end the slave-holders in their war for the perpetuity of slavery and the dissolution of the Union.

The election for governor in the State of Ohio in the fall of 1863 was a striking example of the baneful and deplorable influence of partisan allegiance in carrying thousands of intelligent citizens to the very verge of revolution and rebellion against the authority of their own State. The candidates for governor in that contest, remarkable as a significant event in the history of the period, were John

Brough, Republican, and C. L. Vallandigham, Democrat. Vallandigham was a man of some ready talent and local reputation as a politician in the State. He had been a candidate for a seat in Congress in his own district, and was a delegate to the Democratic Convention which nominated General McClellan for the Presidency. At the opening of the war of the Rebellion he became a violent secessionist, a noisy demagogue of the most offensive type, and so seditious and treasonable was he in language and conduct that he excited among the loyal men of the State the utmost indignation against himself and his associates. The volunteers of the State, both those on duty at the front and those in the home service, were greatly outraged in feeling by his denunciations of themselves as hirelings and cutthroats, and the general government as a despotism of corruption and cruelty. General Burnside was in command of that department at the time, and ordered Vallandigham's arrest and trial by court-martial. He was convicted as charged, and as the shortest and best method of disposing of him he was sent into the Confederate lines. He soon transferred himself into Canada, as it was supposed at the time, that he might better serve the rebel cause and more readily communicate with his political associates and sympathizers. While he was thus on foreign soil, an exile from the State for his treason and sedition against its peace and welfare, with a reputation as odious as that of Benedict Arnold; while the Confederate freebooter, Morgan, was raiding the State with an armed force, and Ohio had one hundred and fifty regiments of volunteers in the field fighting for the life of the nation, this man was nominated in a State convention of Democrats by acclamation. In the resolutions passed by that convention the general government was accused of tyranny and hypocrisy in making war upon the South, a war, it was alleged, that could not, and never was intended to, preserve the Union, but a war to free the blacks by enslaving the whites. Two hundred and fifty thousand Democrats voted for his election while he was yet in Canada, a fugitive from his State. It was one of the most remarkable elections that ever occurred in the history of a free people.

The writer, who was at the time a citizen of the State, well remembers the intense excitement caused by this event throughout the country, and the imminent danger there was for many months that there would be a civil war among the loyal men and the rebel sympathizers in the State. Here was a great war inaugurated in the interests of the system of domestic slavery that then divided and cursed the country, precipitated for the sole purpose of perpetuating the bondage of an unfortunate and helpless race. As a result the union of the States was to be destroyed and the republic divided into two or more hostile sections. What had the free people of Ohio in common with this institution and with such a conspiracy against the peace and general welfare of the nation? Nothing. Slavery was the abhorrence of mankind, a sin against God, and a crime against man; and yet, under the influence of that blind fanaticism which party spirit engenders, thousands of northern citizens gave moral aid and comfort to the Rebellion, from the assault on Fort Sumter to the surrender at Appomattox. It shows the power of party sentiment and discipline in controlling the actions of men who are associated together for a common purpose. What will they not sacrifice to party fealty and party dictation?

CHAPTER V.

PARTIES NEVER DIE.   ALWAYS BE A BAD PARTY.

MANY good citizens, who deplore the evils arising out of the selfishness and greed of party alliances, cherish the hope that as civilization advances, and the world grows wiser and better, the vicious elements in these factions will be eliminated and we shall see patriotism, integrity, and capability exalted in their stead as standard virtues, indispensable to a position in the public service. I do not share with them in this optimistic hope for the future of American politics. Any combination the prime object and business of which is to prey upon the public for the exclusive benefits of its members is, in fact, a public enemy. Every act of such a body in pursuit of its chief designs is a usurpation of authority or a violation of law. When they cease to act they will cease to exist. A thorough house-cleaning would dissolve any of the great political fraternities now in existence, for want of the means of subsistence. With reform would inevitably come the dissolution of the combine. No party, no spoils; no spoils, no party. They are inseparable, and society has no use for either of them.

Again, one reason why there is nothing to hope for from these organizations in the evolution of politics is that they are always, and naturally, formed and built up on the line of social and moral distinctions and differences which determine their character. Hence there will always be a bad party and a better party, comparatively. There will always exist two or more party organizations so long as there is free access to the public crib, a conservative and a progressive organization. One will be exceedingly tenacious of its ancient dogmas and traditions, and will sturdily defend the existing evils of society, and perhaps point with pride to its record as the persistent opponent of the great social and political reforms inaugurated by the people. The other, by a natural antagonism of its rival, will be the champion of all popular reforms, and especially the friend of every man who has a grievance or an empty dinner-pail; while they each employ the same reprehensible devices to secure a common end,—viz., to wrest the government from the hands of the people and place it in the possession of the chief conspirators of their own party, who will distribute its patronage among the lieutenants and bosses of its grand army of occupation.

These confederations, like most other voluntary as-

sociations, are made up of affinities, of persons who
have something in common in the objects of an enterprise, or in whose tastes and general character there
is a similarity and more or less of sympathy.   Persons standing in such relations to one another are apt
to take like views of public questions and party
methods.   The old adage about birds of a feather is
applicable to such political conclaves.   All the business and social unions are composed of persons similar
in their habits, manners, mode of life, and in their
general standing in the community.   Men in forming
such associations seek to bring together congenial
minds.   Every person who joins a club or selects a
place where he will attend religious services on the
Sabbath has a reference to these wise precedents in
exercising a choice of his associates.   For example, Mr.
A is a business man and a respectable, well-to-do citizen of the town; he is a benevolent and perhaps a
religious man.   His chief interest in politics is to see
an honest and clean administration of the affairs of
the government.   He is in favor of free voting and an
honest counting of the results of any election.   All
· the incidents of partisan strife are distasteful to him,
and he seldom "meddles with politics."   Now, this
man feels that in order to discharge his duties as a
citizen he must be found at the polls at every election
and vote conscientiously.   He therefore selects a political organization with which, and through which,
he will act for the best good of his country.   In
making this selection he is influenced by the same considerations that would weigh with him in joining a

religious congregation or a Christian church. He
would associate himself with those who in taste and
character were more in conformity with his own standard of social and religious life.

Mr. B is a differently constituted man; he is neither
as intelligent, as patriotic, nor as kindly disposed towards others as is his neighbor, Mr. A. He is a selfish
man, and has but little interest in anybody beyond the
circle of his own family and kindred. He sees no
reason why contributions should be levied upon him
to support the various projects which charitable people
are always soliciting for, and he rarely does anything
in aid of them. Neither does he see why he should
be taxed for public improvements, which in most cases
benefit others more than himself. His chief interest
in politics, aside from his being a sort of standing candidate for several minor offices, is centred in a few
specialties, which are the cardinal planks in his political platform. These are a low rate of taxation; the
abolition of high salaries for government officials, or
their reduction to his own standard of living; the
right of every man to sell whatever he has produced
or purchased in any quantity and of any quality
wherever there is a demand for it. He is therefore
opposed to all tariffs, all sumptuary laws, and to all
inquisitorial legislation. He is a protectionist in that
he wants his own labor and products protected from
foreign competition; and he is a free-trader in that he
wants placed upon the free list all imported commodities of which he is a consumer. As he has some tene-
ments which he rents to miscellaneous persons, some

of whom are disreputable people, and about whose occupations and vices the police department has given
him some annoyance, he is of the opinion that we are
governed too much, and when the law undertakes
to dictate as to a man's social habits and his business,
it is an undue restraint of his personal liberty. He
religiously believes in the doctrine that to the victor
belong the spoils, and that those who labor in the
political field are worthy of their hire. Now, this
man does not join the same party that Mr. A does.
He says he does not like that sort of a crowd of reformers and radicals. He goes where he can find
more congenial fellowship and a larger degree of personal liberty. He joins the bad party. A becomes a
member of what he calls the best party.

This will be the make-up generally of the two great
parties into which any country may be divided where
free suffrage exists. Such organizations are not, of
course, formed strictly on these lines; there may be
A men in the bad party, and B men in the better
party; and there may be changes and interchanges in
the *personnel* of each body from time to time; but
each association will retain its identity in these respects so long as it holds the same relation to its antagonist. There will always be a bad party so long
as there are bad men and so long as the field of politics is open to such combinations. The faction that
embodies the least intelligence and moral worth in
its membership will draw to it by natural selection
the worst element of the social order. All that class
who are violators of law, whose occupations are at

war with society, who gain their bread by violence or fraud, will seek its protection and ally themselves to its fortunes. Organization enables ambitious and unscrupulous men to mass and keep in training this dangerous political force.

Such a party will be exceedingly tenacious of life and possess an amazing amount of persistence and bull-dog courage. It will be better disciplined, be more bold, unscrupulous, and aggressive in the performance of its chief mission of obtaining spoils for its subsistence and that of its members. For the same reason there will be a strong bond of fraternity among them. As with a band of outlaws, when the service required becomes more hazardous and their violations of law become more frequent and flagrant, the bond of fellowship between them is strengthened, and the general subordination to discipline is more apparent as well as imperative. There is a fellow-feeling among evil-doers that is often more demonstrative and more exemplary than that exhibited in associations of a better class. So long as parties in politics are permitted to exist as contestants for place and power in the public service, so long will there be a vicious party composed chiefly of men who seek first their own advancement and well-being and their country's afterwards.

The disgusted and outraged citizen sometimes finds consolation in the hope that the dominant party, through its inherent corruption and its utter disregard of the public wishes, must soon cease to exist, or to command any respectable following in membership;

and sometimes, when such a party has met a signal defeat in a general election, the cry goes up from the opposing camp, and is echoed over the country, that the great party has made its last campaign, has fought its last battle, and is practically dead. It may be as truly said of political parties as of corporations, that they never die. They may undergo a variety of changes, take on a new name, go into retirement for a period, or form a coalition with a like political force, but they will strive in some form to retain their identity and continue in the competitive race for the spoils of office.

A party is sometimes formed without reference to these rewards for political service. It has at heart what its members deem some measures of public utility which they wish to see put in operation by some appropriate legislation and the election of such citizens as will faithfully administer the laws thus enacted. There may be several branches of reform to which they are directing their efforts. Suppose they are successful in this organization, and obtain such political ascendency that they are able triumphantly to carry all their measures and establish permanently the new conditions they desire, do they thereupon disband the party and cease their labors? Never. There is no such case in the history of politics in this or any other country. They will find new issues with their party opponents and abundant sound and patriotic reasons why they should continue in power indefinitely. The history of the anti-slavery party in this country, inaugurated before the

Rebellion, illustrates the statement. It was an organization formed for the purpose of securing the abolition of American slavery. After varied fortunes it came to be the party in power by the votes of the people, and soon realized its hopes in the abolition of the peculiar institution and the destruction of the slave power, which had ruled the country for half a century or more. But they did not disband after securing the ultimate object of the organization.

We cannot hope to be relieved from the baneful influence of these combinations by the natural decay and inevitable death which is the fate of all other things mundane and organic; they are in the hands of that modern breed of politicians of whom it is said, they never die or resign. So long as the spoils of office are set up by the people as prizes to be won by competing political factions, so long, by the law of supply and demand, will such bodies exist. Where the carcass is, there will the eagles be gathered together. Neither the lapse of time nor the occurrence of the greatest disasters seems materially to affect them. They will live and flourish through years of war, pestilence or famine, as well as long periods of business depression. These public misfortunes generally afford to a party seeking employment for its talents and enterprise a wider field of opportunities for success.

When the corruptions of the Grant administration were revealed to the public, and were universally discussed and condemned by the people, resulting in the nomination of Horace Greeley by the

4

Democratic party as their candidate for the Presidency, there was a great revulsion of sentiment and feeling in the Republican ranks. As a result the Grand Old Party lost thirteen Northern States from its elective force. It was at that time thought by many persons of both parties, and by the Democrats universally, that the organization must succumb to the tide of opposition that threatened to overwhelm it. So when the Democratic party for four years persistently sustained the Southern Rebellion, opposing the war for the restoration of the Union, and giving in a multitude of ways aid and comfort to the enemy, it was universally believed that with a lost cause, ever afterwards to be infamous in history, would be a lost political party to share its fate.

The corruptions of the Tweed administration in the management of the municipal government of the city of New York, twenty years ago, created a profound sensation, and the odium which it brought upon Tammany Hall was supposed to be sufficient to disband and destroy that political faction; but, notwithstanding its past reputation and the more recent exposures of its infamous character, it is still, with its energies and its following scarcely diminished, a powerful political force in the State and city of New York.

No change in the condition of the country that may require a change of public policy, no change of public sentiment, or any effort to reform abuses will materially affect these coalitions, much less close their career and relieve the country of their presence. They thrive on the misfortunes of the commonwealth and rise elastic from their own defeats and disasters. When such an organization has once gained ascendency and has tasted the sweets of office and the luxury of power, it never goes into voluntary retirement or formally disbands. It may be merged with some other rising and kindred organization, but it will not intentionally commit suicide. There may be an infusion of other blood into the new combination, and its members may heed for a time the admonition of an indignant people, but the old passion for place and power will have but a temporary decline and will inevitably revive in the presence of the old temptations. It will be a change only of party name, which may result in a change of tactics and the lopping off of a few old abuses. The fresh element will be more greedy for spoils, though perhaps less unscrupulous in the pursuit of them. The betterment will only be spasmodic and temporary, and no permanent reform will be made. There will be the same prizes to be won by hard contests with rival factions, and the same party necessity for obtaining them. Such combinations will always exist, unless prohibited by law. So long as power and plunder can be obtained and honors won in a bloodless strife of factions for political ascendency, so long will organizations of this character rule the country, endangering its liberties and despoiling its resources.

CHAPTER VI.

DISPARAGEMENT OF PUBLIC MEN. HAVE WE ANY GREAT MEN ?

The degrading influence of party rivalry and strife is signally manifest in the license of the partisan press, as well as of individuals, in their treatment of persons in public positions. In no part of the civilized world, perhaps, is there so little respect paid to those who hold places of honor and trust under governments, State or national, as in our own country. As soon as a man is known to be a candidate for public office he becomes, temporarily at least, a target for all the slings and arrows of party animosity far and near. If he is elected by the people to fill the place he seeks, this hostile attitude towards him will be maintained and intensified to the end of his official career. It seems a perversion of all justice and propriety that in the land where all the people are acknowledged sovereigns, and there are no subjects and no tyrants, those we choose to represent us in civil affairs should be objects of persistent disparagement and ridicule.

There is no position with which a citizen may be honored by the choice and consent of the people in which he will be free from this shameful annoyance and party persecution. These persons are chosen to the places they occupy by a majority of their fellow-citizens, which means practically, in a representative

government like our own, by the choice and consent
of all the people. Such a man is your representative
and mine, whatever the difference may be politically
between us, or whether we voted for him or a defeated candidate. Because he does not, as he could
not, represent the opinions of everybody in the district, a majority of his constituents even would have
no right to annoy him on such grounds. To adopt
such a rule in the support of public men would dissolve the bonds of civilized society and render the
maintenance of civil government impossible. If to
be chosen by one's fellow-citizens to a place of trust
and power in a commonwealth is not an honor conferred upon the recipient of such confidence and
authority, entitling him to respect in his official capacity, then it is because the government whose
power he wields is not entitled to the respect and
confidence of other civil states.

It has become a confirmed habit of the American
people, as individual partisans, to regard the man who
holds a prominent position in public life, and who is
active and earnest in supporting his party creed and
measures, as a sort of public enemy, and in a great
measure to treat him as such. The opposing factions
to which he does not belong will gather up all the incidents of his private life and his family connections,
his idiosyncrasies, personal habits and tastes, as well
as those of his political career and aspirations, and out
of the record select such facts and happenings as may
be used to disparage him and show if possible that he
is unworthy of the confidence of the people, and unfit

or incompetent to hold the place he occupies. Grave
charges against such a man or an investigation of his
conduct gives nobody pangs but his friends. It will
prove a sensation in any community which the majority of the people of all parties will quite enjoy.
The newspapers, in giving details of the scandal as it
develops, will have a profitable and busy run of the
press. There will be a general conviction not unlikely
in the community, in advance of the proper verdict,
that he is guilty as charged. When party animosity
becomes personal it soon comes to be slanderous,
libellous, and scandalous, and it would be scarcely restrained from assuming a more violent form of malev-
olence and hostility, were it not for the sense of justice
and propriety among those citizens who have no other
than a patriotic interest in our current politics.

Hero worship and tuft-hunting are not social vices
with which the American people can be charged to
any extent. We are therefore in danger of going to
the opposite extreme, in habitual disparagement of
those whom impartial men the world over delight to
honor as distinguished American citizens. That this
want of due respect for public men, even those of the
highest character and most distinguished ability, is
due to partisan antipathy and education I have no
doubt. That it has become general among our people
cannot be denied. We have a large class of publica-
tions in various forms, some of them of a partisan
character, and others claiming to be neutral in politics, which are devoted largely to this reprehensible
business of assailing in various ways the acts and good

name of our public men. Some of these enterprising citizens make it their sole business to cater to depraved public taste in this respect. These assaults are personal in their character, and are scarcely less injurious and unlawful often than a more violent attack would be, accompanied with battery. The victims of these aggravated assaults are caricatured in every form which art and ingenuity can command, and often in the grossest and most repulsive manner. A President of the republic, a cabinet officer, or some other distinguished statesman will be pictorially represented in a score of disgusting and derisive forms; he may be made to represent a beast, a foul bird, or a reptile monster, as the distempered fancy of the author may dictate. It is much to be regretted that men who have the inventive genius and skill evinced in these impersonations should lend themselves to this dirtiest of partisan work.

These caricatures are placed conspicuously in the shop windows and nailed upon the door-posts of the news-dealers, and the people hasten to purchase them, while the poorer class of citizens obstruct the foot-way in the street in their eagerness to enjoy what they deem a good practical joke upon the victim of this outrage. This partisan method of making political capital and sustaining the doctrine of rotation in office has become a species of popular amusement, and a thriving trade to those who cater to this morbid taste. There are many reputable citizens who laugh with the multitude over these political persecutions, and in many ways countenance and aid in this annoyance and defamation of character, who would very speedily resort to the law, or an act of personal violence, if they or their families were made victims of such wanton calumny and ridicule. These demoralizing incidents show to what extent the party strife may deprave the morals and taste of an intelligent and Christian people.

During the administration of General Grant as President there came to Washington from the West a dissipated and broken-down politician in search of a job. He was not long in getting control of a moribund Sunday newspaper of small circulation, with a purpose of devoting its columns almost exclusively to libellous and indecent attacks upon public men, and more especially upon senators and representatives in Congress, and upon the President and his cabinet. These gentlemen he naturally supposed would take no public notice of his productions in print, and would not be likely to call him to account for his shameless effrontery and ill-breeding. From their public positions they were non-combatants, and must maintain the silence of contempt as their only defense. Cowards and unscrupulous knaves seek such victims in their predatory excursions for notoriety and their daily bread. This man had a degree of low comedy talent and its boon companions garrulity and wit, with all the unbounded assurance and self-esteem of the pothouse politician. His scurrilous attacks upon public men, from their audacity, soon attracted general attention, and his Sunday paper was much in demand. Everybody was curious to know who was assailed in

each issue of the sheet, and speculation was rife as
to the temper in which these poisoned arrows would
be received by those at whom they were aimed, and
what would be the consequences to the culprit of such
an impudent and outrageous onslaught upon public
functionaries in high position.

The offence was almost unprecedented at the
national capitol. The Washington press from time
immemorial had treated each succeeding administration with marked toleration and respect. The citizens of Washington have always been distinguished
for the deference and hospitality with which they
have treated the large body of official persons residing temporarily in their midst. Reports were current that blackmail was being levied on a class of
vulnerable people to exempt them from criticism or
exposure, and that the increasing amount of adver-
tising matter in that journal was obtained through
the same agency. Ladies in official circles became
very sensitive and not a little alarmed on seeing their
husbands and fathers so ruthlessly assailed, and had
reasonable apprehensions for their own safety from
similar outrage. The matter became one of the sen-
sations of the town, and threatened to be an absorbing one.

Though this disturber of the public peace had no
recognized standing as a politician, or rank as a
partisan, he had acquired some experience of the political changes occurring during his voting majority.
He was at one time a Whig, afterwards a Know-
nothing, and then a Republican. At the time of his

advent into Washington life he was a Democrat.
Under cover of party opposition to the Administration, General Grant was specially the object of his
malevolent and cowardly aggressions, in which the
members of his family were frequently included.
The President was caricatured, ridiculed, and represented in the most persistent and offensive manner.
The party press in different parts of the country
copied many of these ribald effusions, and the matter threatened to become a national scandal. Sober
and law-abiding citizens began to feel that some
measures more speedy than libel-suits should be
adopted to abate the nuisance. These attacks at
length became so personal and so insulting to the
Presidential office and the occupants of the White
House that Colonel Fred. Grant was stirred to decisive action in the matter. It is known that about this
time he visited the house of the offending editor, in
company with a young army officer who was a friend
of the colonel, and it is said that he intended to give
the libeller of his family a thrashing suitable to his
offences and his general character; but the object of
this morning call was fortunate enough to make his
escape out of the back door of his castle before his
visitors caught sight of him.

Meantime, it was reported that several senators
were on the war-path. Senator Zack Chandler was
said to be hunting the avoidant editor with a large
hickory walking-stick, and others were impatiently
waiting an opportunity to give him a caning. In
consequence of these demonstrations there was an

immediate change in the character of the next issue of the Sunday sheet, as well as thereafter. The public nuisance was effectually abated, and the author of it all at length disappeared from the national capital together with the terrible stench he had created. There was much in the administration of President Grant that invited criticism and that was very generally condemned, but there was no good grounds for such aspersions upon his character and fame.

Such a scandal would not be tolerated in any country in the civilized world. No barbarous nation, unless rife for revolution or rebellion, would offer such indignities to their men and rulers.

A similar persistent attempt was made to degrade the character and destroy the influence of Mr. Lincoln as the chief executive of the nation. A powerful minority of partisans had been educated into the belief that he was a selfish demagogue, and was promoting the Civil War relentlessly for the purpose of ambition, rather than a patriotic desire to maintain the integrity of the Union. His assassin was trained for the crime he committed, and stimulated for the hour and the act of his commission by these multiplied and oft-repeated slanders of a great and good man.

Our late President, Mr. Cleveland, was persecuted for four years with the same disgraceful tactics. He was not charged with any offences against law or the morals of society. His chief culpability, that the nation at large had any interest in, was his adherence to the principals and platform of his

party. To this partisans could not consistently object, though they did, however, and all the political
factions of the country made common cause in this
unprecedented crusade against a chief magistrate for
being a too conspicuous and persistent partisan.

It is gratifying to know that the public mind is
not wholly insensible to the many evils arising out
of this mischievous and libellous crusade against
law-abiding citizens. I see that a member of the
New York Senate has recently introduced a bill in
that body making it a criminal offence to thus injure
the standing and caricature the person of any citizen
of the State. The weak defence often made by persons engaged in this sort of calumny, that they bear
no malice towards their *victims*, and are only pleas-
antly chaffing them for their own good and the
amusement of the public, strongly reminds me of
what Solomon says of the man who casts firebrands,
arrows, and death about him and asserts that he is
only in sport. Another will seek to justify this
reprehensible practice by alleging that it is a very
convenient method of enforcing many valuable
truths that would otherwise not reach the popular
mind. This is the doctrine of political Jesuits, that
the end justifies the means.

As a nation we have cultivated that sort of famili-
arity with those we are bound to honor which is said
to breed contempt. We apply to them the question-
able and paradoxical epithet of servants, meaning
that they are persons who work for the people for a
consideration. You will sometimes hear a citizen

speak contemptuously of the incumbent of an office
as nothing but a hired man in the public service. It
is a common occurrence that official persons in the
highest positions will speak of themselves and others
in like circumstances as public servants, or sign
themselves "Your humble servant." Society the
world over requires a social distinction between servants and gentlemen. If such a distinction has any
warrant in the social order, it would be well to give
our citizens eminent in civil affairs the benefit of it.
This habit of contemplating our statesmen and
rulers from so low a point in the social scale is probably due to party subserviency and the arts of the
demagogues in endeavoring to catch votes. It is a
stooping to conquer, a sop to the Cerberus of poverty
and labor. The word servant is a correlative of master, mistress, and employer, and implies inferiority
of station and submission to the will of another for a
stipulated price.

A public officer may be the servant of a despot or
king, who creates and controls the official place he
occupies at his will, but ours is a representative government. The citizens of an election district, for
example, choose one of their number to go on business for them to the State or the national legislature, to represent them in the assembly which makes
the laws governing the country. If it were practicable we would each of us go to the same place.
That would be true democracy. But as it is not possible to do the business of a great nation in this cumbrous and expensive manner, we select men from

the district or State in which we live to represent us
there, and perform for us, at their discretion, such
acts as in their judgment may be for the best interests of themselves and their constituents. This
selection and this discretion, and the power with
which we intrust them, implies our confidence in
them, and is a testimonial to their general character
and fitness for the duties they are chosen to perform.
Such a delegate acts for himself in the legislative
body, and is the representative and proxy of a portion of his fellow-citizens. These persons are the
representatives and not the servants of the people.
They are not laborers for hire, and do not serve their
constituents in that capacity. These distinctions are
fundamental in civil government and in society generally, and cannot be ignored. If they are not,
honor and station in any sphere of human activity
are not worth the seeking.

In a like spirit of disparaging criticism, we hear
people complain that there are no great men in public life at the present time. Their ideals of distinguished men are all in the talking statesmen of the
past. They have seen the present generation of public functionaries so assaulted and pursued, so libelled
and caricatured, during their whole career that they
have little or no respect for any of them. Who can
make a hero out of his servant, or a great man out
of one whom he sees held up constantly to ridicule
and contempt and charged with a great variety of
offences against society and those who have reposed
confidence in him? It is not in human nature that

we can sincerely honor and respect a man who is personally a stranger to us when our daily paper is constantly sneering at his talents and general ability, and our nearest neighbor is confidently assuring us almost daily that the accused is a selfish demagogue, and is unworthy of the public confidence and support. Men nowadays seldom speak of their political representatives other than in a mood of suspicion and criticism. And yet there never was a larger number of able and patriotic men in public life in this country than there are to-day. For practical statesmanship, for wide experience in civil affairs, for learning and ability in the discharge of their onerous duties, there are a large number of them who well deserve the encomiums of the people and the appellation of great men. There are a score of great men in the American Congress at this hour who would distinguish themselves in any legislative body, or in the performance of any service their country might require of them at home or abroad. Deplorably as our Congress has been handicapped and distracted by party strife for the last thirty years, it has not been excelled in any country, or in any age, in the number of wise and patriotic men eminently qualified to make the laws and shape the public policy of a great nation, notwithstanding it is the fashion to decry and caricature them with little discrimination.

The arena of party politics is not a sphere favorable to the development of great and noble qualities in men. It is not an atmosphere in which statesman-

ship and the higher purposes of civil administration
may be fostered and find moral support. Such an
environment is suited rather to the breeding of that
swarm of bosses, demagogues, and political shysters
which so largely control the political situation in
every State of the Union. And yet we have statesmen in spite of their adverse surroundings. There
are men and women in almost every community, be
it said in charity to our common nature, of such high
endowment that they are above gross temptation in
any sphere of life; like Milton's Abdiel, they grow
sterner and stronger under the seductive arts of the
wicked. The national civil service should be an appropriate training-school for those who are ambitious of distinction in the public service, but a partisan conspiracy has degraded it to a competitive
rivalry of contending factions for place and power.
This repels men of character and worth who are ambitious of high repute in the administration of civil
affairs. Partisan rule has debased the standard by
which great public services should be estimated, and
has taught the nation to applaud and respect the
assumptions and political fallacies of demagogues
and charlatans. The people have little use for the
time-honored statesmen of other days. They prefer
to follow the lead of those who are eloquent in de-
picting the alleged poverty and suffering of the
masses and the arrogance and oppression of what
they call the classes. They want patrons who hold
the wand of accomplishment in their hands and can
change the destiny of the nation at their will.

Whatever promises a political sensation and a change of party rule finds abundant following. The men who think, the men who are deliberate and prudent in their action in the direction and management of public affairs, are not in demand by the great mass of those who wield the elective franchise; they want immediate action on every question of importance to the public, and are impatient of any delay. They want those who represent them to do their thinking while on their legs, and lose no time in bringing in the promised political millenium.

Who does not know that this state of the country is largely due to the teachings of that school of politics in which we have all been educated; teachings which have a tendency to degrade the public morals and debase and distract the civil service. This national policy of party rule, unfortunately adopted by our people, and by which the country is divided and governed by constantly recurring factions, is the bane of the republic. This is what so many honest and patriotic citizens symbolize as "the dirty waters of politics," a Stygian pool whose waters soil everything they touch.

CHAPTER VII.

PARTY METHODS. CARRYING ELECTIONS.

THE chief ground of complaint heard on every hand against current political parties is the corrupt methods they put to use in obtaining power and in maintaining their ascendency while in possession of the government. I shall refer briefly to some of the more common expedients resorted to by the political craftsmen of the present time, avoiding that much-explored field of facts and incidents with which the partisan press has already made the world familiar.

It is with some reluctance that I direct the attention of the reader to the means which these fraternities commonly employ in the pursuit of their objects of association as a political party. The subject is a hackneyed one in the literature of politics, and in its details there is much that is repulsive and painful to the friends of free institutions and public virtue. Without some review of this wide field of partisan activity I cannot do justice to myself or to the general subject I have undertaken to discuss. The means and measures adopted by an individual in the management of his business, or of any special enterprise, are generally regarded as pretty sure indications, if not complete tests, of his general character. These decide the question of his general reputation and his standing as a citizen. If he is selfish, exclusive, bigoted, and intolerant in his intercourse with his neighbors; if in his business methods he is unscrupulous and mendacious; if he habitually disregards the rights and opinions of others, and in pursuit of his ends will violate law, and commit crime even, when he can do it with impunity, society will regard him with distrust and avoid him as a person unfit to share the confidence and respect of honorable men. The generally accepted rule that a man's acts are a true test of his character is quite as applicable to associate bodies of every order as to individuals. We have very high authority for saying that "by their fruits ye shall know them."

By the aid of time and experience the modern spoilsmen have brought into use a multitude of skilful devices through which the dynasty of partisan politics has become the supreme power in every state and county in the Federal Union. Many of these artifices of modern statesmanship are of a nature utterly subversive of civil liberty and the primary rights of citizenship. Of these, none are more repugnant to free institutions, or hostile to the liberties of the people, than the methods they employ in manipulating the votes of the country and controlling all elections by the people. To deprive a citizen of his vote is to take away his birthright and rob him of his sovereignty. The right to vote is the most sacred franchise the citizen can enjoy; to defraud him of it by any device should be declared a crime in every civilized country. But who does not know that the violation of this right is recognized by the political parties as one of the great agencies of success in carrying popular elections. To them the selection of candidates for office is a matter of chief consideration. By controlling the party nominations they have the means of rewarding the services of those who are useful to them, and at the same time filling all the official places with men loyal to the party, and who will make the interest of the joint concern their first duty under all circumstances. They begin their labors at the very sources of political power in the country,—the primary meetings of the people preparatory to an election.

The first step taken in this conspiracy to defeat a free and deliberate choice of candidates by the people is the assembling of the caucus of the party leaders of the township or ward. At this caucus a ticket is made up, to be presented at the primary meeting near at hand to select delegates for the county or city convention. The persons who attend this caucus and prepare this list of delegates are generally the local office-holders of the ward or township, with a sprinkling of contractors, small traders, saloon-keepers, and boss mechanics. While none of them may be men of bad repute, they are on the whole a miscellaneous crowd of persons who make political preferment a trade, and who are known as the most subservient and faithful tools of the party to which they belong. They are sometimes designated as strikers, healers, and bosses by the partisan press, if they are adherents of a rival organization. This ticket is brought into the primary meeting, composed generally in the rural districts and smaller towns of such citizens as are known members of the party who may choose to come.

On the day when the primary meeting is held in the district in which you reside, Mr. A and several gentlemen, tax-payers who have a patriotic interest in the administration of public affairs, go to the meeting for the purpose of exerting their influence and casting their votes in favor of some local reforms that are in general demand by the public. They find, when the meeting is called to order, that it is in the hands of a class of ward or town politicians, who dictate and control entirely its actions. Instead of its being an assemblage of citizens to discuss questions of public policy and the merits of candidates, they find that all such action is forestalled by the circulation of a ticket made up in the caucus, and that the meeting is in the control of those who have dictated it. This caucus ticket is put to vote and elected as speedily as possible, and an adjournment is hastened, *sine die.* This same method, with some modifications, is adopted in the county and State conventions for the election of delegates who are to nominate the persons who are to fill all official places. The ticket is "cut and dried" and "put through" under the strictest party discipline, and the man who refuses to acquiesce in this nefarious job will forfeit his standing in the party, and will be denounced as a bolter and an impracticable, who is not wanted in the organization.

This system, by which a small minority of voters become the proxies of a whole community in casting

their ballots, has been carried to a high degree of efficiency in this country, so that it is almost automatic in its action, a sort of self-moving instrumentality that does its work with very little friction or delay. It is a part of the modern tactics by which an oligarchy of politicians and place-brokers are enabled to rule the country by the tacit consent of the people, and is collectively known as machine politics. The packing of the primaries in the large cities and towns is a scheme resorted to by the party bosses to maintain discipline and secure a solid vote in every emergency.

No man can be admitted to this cabal of intriguers who has the reputation of having a tender conscience or being a scrupulously honest man. A man may be a good Republican or Democrat, but he cannot have a vote in the primary meeting unless he is a member of the organization who has been admitted under a blackball test and is thus vouched for by the party managers. The great mass of the voters in these districts are practically disfranchised by this combination of conspirators. Said Governor Markham, of our own State, California, in a message to the Legislature on this subject, "The danger to our government lies in the loose and very often profligate manner in which these elections are conducted, regardless of the rights of communities, imperilling their safety, and entirely under the control of the worst elements of society. Like stringent laws, which protect the voter at a regular election, should shield him at the primaries. It is absurd to declare that the voter has the right at a general election to vote for whom he pleases, when those for whom he must vote have been placed before him without giving him an opportunity of declaring his choice. The privilege of nomination is strangled at the birth, and he must follow the dictates of a convention corruptly assembled, or quietly abstain from the use of the franchise. This is an evil growing by what it feeds on, threatening the liberties of the people by debarring them from the free and untrammelled exercise of personal choice."

The rules of Tammany Hall for many years past have made the consent of a majority of the members of each primary necessary to the admission of a new member. A similar system is in use by the Republican party in that city. The organization of one hundred and twenty-four Republican primaries (one for each assembly district) is as strict as that of a private club. The name of the applicant must be posted on a bulletin and stand for inspection until the next monthly meeting before it can go to the committee on admissions. On a favorable report it must have a majority at the monthly meeting. If accepted, he must pledge himself to obey all orders of the General Committee and to support all nominations approved by that committee—this is a rule of both parties; he must bind himself not to join any organization which does not recognize the authority of the association he joins. He may be expelled at any time by a vote of the majority of the members.

In 1880 it was computed that out of fifty-eight thousand Republican votes in New York City, not more than six or eight hundred were members of the organization and entitled to vote in the primaries. The members present in the primaries are always noticeably small. In 1888 only about eight per cent. of the Republican electors took part in the primary election. In only eight out of twenty-four districts did the percentage exceed ten, and in some it was as low as two per cent. In the Twenty-first Assembly District Tammany Primary, one hundred and sixteen delegates to choose an assembly candidate were elected by less than fifty votes. In the Sixth Assembly District County Democracy Primary, less than seven per cent. of Democratic voters were present; of those who were, sixty-nine were election officers. These devices indicate a deliberate plan on the part of the political directors and spoilsmen of the party to place its power under their control exclusively. Yea, more, it proves them guilty of a conspiracy to place its direction and management beyond the control of the people. A party formed for such purposes, whose aims are hostile to the general welfare, cannot tolerate the presence and interference of scrupulous and over-sensitive men.

CHAPTER VIII.

ELECTION METHODS CONTINUED.

THIS is the preparation they make for what is called an election of the people, and it is by similar methods that such elections are carried. The party devices for carrying popular elections are almost countless in number. They are so minute and ingenious in their application that they cover the whole field of operation as with a net-work, laid to ensnare the enemy and capture neutrals. We have, in this country, where many of these devices originated, acquired such proficiency in the use of them, and they have so long been tolerated, that they are regarded abroad as the natural appendages and offshoots of our free institutions. They have chiefly found development in the great cities of the country where there are brought to bear upon their success the sagacity and experience of all the politicians for a century past. In these great centres of political activity they have been reduced to a system of discipline and subordination which defies all authority, civil or religious.

There is quite a catalogue of these party tactics, each bearing a familiar name by which they are known and recognized throughout the country, such as bulldozing, colonizing, corralling, sweating, shooting, hanging, kidnapping, false registering, repeating, bribing, assault and battery, perjury, discharging

from employment, lying, counting out, riots, threats
of violence, notice to leave the country, refusing cer-
tificates to candidates elected and granting them to
persons not elected, holding over, contesting seats,
falsifying and stealing election returns. Added to
these are a large number of devices used in immediate connection with the preparation, depositing,
and counting of ballots cast. A political boss or
striker who is expert in these machinations will play
more tricks with a ballot-box and a few hundred
votes than an Eastern juggler can with a pack of
cards. These discreditable practices, with a multitude of others that might be named, indicate the
great variety and general character of the methods
employed by the great parties in carrying the more
important of our elections, State or national.

Fraud, violence, and intimidation prevail more or
less in every important election. Men of a certain
class are trained to this work, and such only are employed as are skilful and unscrupulous in the performance of it. These men, many of them, go
armed to the polling places, ostensibly for the purpose of protecting themselves from assaults of the
strikers and henchmen of the opposing party. Each
party has its corps of solicitors, challengers, detectives, and fighting men. They must each make a
show of force and courage against what they call the
bravado and bullying of the opposite faction. Both
sides must be aggressive and confident, and maintain
their rights and their strategic positions at the polling places at any cost. In the cities it requires the

presence of an armed police force to maintain order and prevent bloodshed between the contending factions, and not unfrequently a military force is in waiting under arms in case of emergency, so that an election is sometimes turned into riot, and the town assumes a warlike appearance.

Election day in a great city is more or less a day of excitement and apprehension, a day of accidents and incidents, a day when the worst elements are abroad and the most dangerous forces of society are brought into close and antagonizing proximity. On this eventful day the chief of police will have his force well in hand, for nobody knows what may happen. If there are no assaults with battery and bloodletting, no violations of law, murder, or manslaughter, citizens say, with a feeling of relief, that the election has passed off quietly and that they are glad that the campaign is over.

During the session of the New York Legislature of 1894, there came to that body from the city of Troy, on the Hudson River, loud complaints of outrages, involving murder and other high crimes, committed in connection with recent elections in that city. The State Senate appointed a committee to investigate and report upon the facts in the case. This report, though it deals with and censures but a small number of these outrages against a helpless minority, is sufficient to give us some idea of the condition of lawlessness into which the country is drifting under partisan violence and misrule. We quote from this report as follows:

"The history of these two elections (November, 1893, and March, 1894) presents a shocking condition of affairs. It shows uniform and intentional violations of nearly every provision of the election laws, and constant interference with and outrage upon the rights of the public and of honest citizens. It is a story of repeating, violence, rioting, and crime culminating in murder. It is the exemplified work of a desperate and hitherto resistless political machine, so adjusted, organized, and run as to enable individuals in the name of the Democratic party and in defiance of law to overthrow government and thwart the rights of suffrage. This machine is an organization composed of professional politicians, having a recognized, acknowledged, and responsible head, and operates through Democratic election officers, repeaters, and other outlaws, supported by a police department and a police force obedient to its dictation. It attracts and unites to itself the criminal class, and its election-day work is done by heelers and desperadoes, some of whom serve as election officers, others as police, and the balance as repeaters under the guidance of the first two. This organization, known as the 'Murphy Machine,' approves, rewards, and protects its tools, and thus perpetuates its power. The process known as 'repeating' is accomplished by persons not entitled to vote going through the city singly or in bands, voting in the various districts on the names of legally registered voters. In many instances and in many districts names of persons legally entitled to vote were voted upon two or three or more times during one election. Sometimes the legal voter, whose name was given to a repeater, would at the time be in the line and would himself protest against the outrage. In such case the legal voter would be threatened with arrest by a Democratic policeman for disturbing the election; and when such legal voter was finally allowed to cast his vote he invariably had to swear it in. Police officers, aldermen, and other officials piloted and protected this disreputable gang in this damnable business from polling place to polling place in the city. A sergeant of police, an ex-president of the Common Council, a member of the detective force are samples of the official positions held by those who escorted and guarded these criminals in the commission of their crimes. Upon reaching a polling place the voting thugs would be taken in charge by the official thugs in a blacksmith's-shop, a saloon, or other convenient place, and the official or other worker having these in charge would enter the polling place and obtain from a Democratic inspector a list of unvoted names, or the worker would himself carry the registry list out of the polling place and make the list himself, and upon the names so obtained the waiting repeater would, upon receiving his name, enter and vote. In not one case was a gang of repeaters headed by a Republican. In not one case was a challenge interposed by a Democrat. In not a single case was a repeater arrested by a Democratic policeman; and we recollect no case in which a Republican challenge was not overruled by the Democratic majority. Repeated requests to arrest these criminals were made to the police by the Republicans, but no arrests were made; and the only person in danger of arrest was the person making the request."）

These are not exclusively the methods in use by any single party, though our Democratic guardians of the Constitution and the public service may excel all others in the practice of these lawless acts. There is an old adage that when rogues fall out

honest men come at the truth. This is often verified when the parties make investigation and report
upon one another's conduct in relation to public
affairs, so that much that is said and proved as to
their corrupt practices is derived from investigations
held upon the ways and means of each other's stewardship. From its partisan character it may be
taken with allowance, but with all such charitable
discount we have enough in evidence to prove the
infamous character of these organizations. Take
the reports of Congressional committees and committees of State Legislatures on the question of contested seats, and you will have the most indis-
putable evidence that violence and fraud are the
commonest agencies in use by all the political partisans in carrying elections all over the country.

I do not affirm that all the elections held in our
extended domain are characterized by these reprehensible tactics, with which the citizens of Troy
were made familiar. They are not. A large
majority of them are conducted, so far as the polling
places are concerned, in a quiet and orderly manner,
with no visible signs of disorder or party animosity.
These popular assemblages have improved in these
respects very decidedly in the last twenty-five years.
While the parties have changed for the better somewhat in their public demonstrations, they manifest
no improvement whatever in their chief purpose and
general character. During this period named they
have been gradually but surely acquiring possession

and control of all the political forces of the republic, until they are well-nigh absolute in their dominion over the nation.

CHAPTER IX.

PURCHASING VOTES.

TRADING in votes is another very considerable factor in gaining a fraudulent election. Counterfeiting tickets, and selling out one candidate for the benefit of another, with many other devices of a kindred sort, are very generally in vogue; but the chief business in this line of traffic is in the actual purchase of votes, or the hiring of electors for a consideration to cast their ballots for certain persons. This infamous commerce, from its secret and confidential nature, is much larger than is generally supposed. Those persons who deal in contraband or prohibited goods must sell by samples generally and have visible stocks on hand, and are thus constantly liable to detection; but those engaged in this peculiar traffic are not subject to such risk and and exposure. This vice has never made its appearance in this country in such frequency as to attract public attention until within the period of the present generation, since which it has become, in some of the older States, one of the recognized methods of the parties in carrying elections.

In conversing with a gentleman who resides in

the State of New York, at a county seat on the Hudson River, he said that it is well understood in his section of the State that votes were bought and sold at any important election. [He said, "I have often seen the old farmers sitting on the fences at the polling places late in the day driving cash bargains with the politicians for their votes." These men who had votes to sell were, he said, chiefly of foreign birth, and he believed the vice had been imported into this country with an immigrant farming and laboring population. Whatever its origin, it is undoubtedly true, as we have charged, that a growing traffic of this sort has been established, and is fostered and in use by the political parties for their advantage. Everybody knows that whenever there is an individual or an association who has votes to sell, at wholesale or retail, they will find a ready market for them, and some active competition among buyers of the partisan sort. It is a most degrading form of avarice, and it seems almost incredible that any man bred amid the monuments of freedom could so disgrace and emasculate himself.[It is a crime worse than that of Esau. Such a person is not fit to exercise the high privileges of American citizenship, and he should be forever disfranchised.

[There is another still more reprehensible practice, if possible, arising from the same source. I allude to the procurement of the votes of unnaturalized foreigners at the elections in towns and cities. The great parties are always hunting for votes, and will obtain them by almost any device or at any cost.

The large body of immigrants constantly landing in our cities afford a field of enterprise for this scandalous traffic. From the desire of the parties to make the immigrant vote available as soon as possible, and a further desire to gain the favor and patronage of this class, they have caused the period of probation which each new-comer must pass to be reduced to an inconsiderable space of time. Not content with this, they provide him often with fraudulent naturalization papers and declare him a legal voter before he has been a month in the country.) This nefarious practice is one of the greatest of the many outrages practised upon the American people, by fraudulent and hasty introduction of this base and perjured element into our politics.

The public sentiment of this country will welcome to our shores every man, of whatever nationality, who will become a good citizen, but they do object, as some one has said, to the making of our towns and villages dumping-grounds for the human garbage of European cities. Many of this purchasable class are fugitives from justice, discharged convicts, and persons who have been sent out of the country for their country's good by the courts and various social and religious societies. This element, by party tactics, is fraudulently injected into our political system, and these men, fresh from the slums of Europe, are immediately placed upon a political equality with American citizens whose fathers first made this country habitable,

6

gained its independence, and planted it with free institutions.

Here is a despatch from the Associated Press, which is quite significant of the activity of this business on the Pacific coast. It is headed,—

"NATIVE SONS WITH PIGTAILS WHO WILL DABBLE
IN POLITICS.

"SAN FRANCISCO, April 6.

"A political club is being formed in this city by several Chinese who have the right to vote, and the bosses behind it expect to make it several hundred strong by the next election. Ning Gun and Loeng Chung, two native-born Chinese, have established head-quarters on Clay street, where they have installed a political club under the guise of Native Sons. On the door is a sign reading, 'Chinese Native Sons' Association, Confucius Parlor.' This club numbers at present about fifty members, and there are said to be two thousand American-born Chinese here that are entitled to vote and who will join the club.

"About fifty Chinese voted at the last election, and the Australian ballot has no terrors for them. Practical politicians are scheming as to the possibility of buying Chinese votes in blocks of two thousand and utilizing them in a manner that will overthrow any majority that white American citizens may give a candidate."

The more shrewd and intelligent of this class, from the favor with which they are received, have taken up the trade of politics, and they constitute in some of our large cities almost the entire force of municipal bosses, party managers, and office-holders. It is said that in Boston ninety-five per cent. of the officials and employees of the city are of foreign birth. As a general thing, in all our northern cities the ward bosses and bullies were reared on the other side of the Atlantic. I cannot perhaps do better in sustaining my views of this branch of the general subject than to conclude it by quoting an editorial from a leading foreign journal, the Glasgow *Evening News.* Its text is the word "Boss," a theme which it discusses in this free and earnest style:

["Although the word 'boss' is so familiar as to have secured the respectful recognition of the latest lexicographers, it does not figure even in the slang dictionaries of ten years ago. It has come to us from the Americans, who got it from the Dutch (*baas,* a master), and is to-day in Britain the brief synonyme for a superintendent in all ranks) from navvying to banking. But while Britain uses the word 'boss' in a cheerful and flippant spirit, the Americans have infused it with a meaning far deeper, far more serious, then we can readily understand. The 'Boss' (for he is considered worthy of a capital B now in the States) has become one of the most extraordinary features, if not the most extraordinary feature, of American municipal life, and 'Bossing' is a disease which is eating into the vitals of American citizenship. The Boss of the United States, from New York to San Francisco, is Irish,—not the decent, warm-hearted, hospitable, honest Irish to be met with (maugre Home Rule agitations) in Kerry or in Clare, but the ignorant, blatant, plug-ugly Hibernian who is a cross between the scum of Dublin City and the sweepings of the Bowery. Bred in the odor

of the saloons and the gambling-hells, he graduates
in time to the domination of other 'patriotic exiles,'
and practically owns the polling booths of the municipal wards. An Irishman has no sooner landed off
the ship and set foot on Castle Garden, than the Boss
has him under his thumb by bribery, by threat, or
by the old inalienable claim of clanship, so strong a
factor in bringing the Celtic races to the front.
There landed in America from Ireland during the
past half-century no less than three million two
hundred and fifty thousand Irish people, and the
sons of this great multitude, native-born, have shown
a marvellous hereditary aptitude for securing offices,
such as those of alderman, councilman, policeman,
bureau chief, and mayor. When they are not
bribing their way to office, they are breeding Irish
voters, with the result that so long ago as 1886 more
than a seventh of the entire population of the city
of New York was of Irish birth. New York is under the heel of the Irish Boss. It is a fact apparent
in the press of the State, and more especially in the
illustrated comic journals, such as *Life* and *Judge*,
which have for years made sarcastic capital out of
the tyrannous Hibernian 'copper,' the vulgar and
ignorant Hibernian alderman, and the thieving Hibernian public contractor. The men who control the
affairs of New York are pure Irish. Its mayor, city
chamberlain, president of the Board of Police Commissioners, police court judges, chief criminal judge,
superintendent of the public force, etc., form one of
the most remarkable oligarchies ever known, and the
simple reading of the roll of officials of the Empire
City, with its Gilroys, Fitzgeralds, Sullivans, Sheas,
Murphys, Ryans, and Burkes, would 'send a thrill
of joy through the bones of the Irish kings.' If New
York was well governed there would not be the same
ground for alarm at this universal rule of the Irish

minority; but it is not well governed. The officials filch the rate-payers' money on all hands,—witness the present John Y. McKane scandal in the Gravesend suburb,—and corruption penetrates to the very heart of a municipality which has ceased to be an edifying study for municipal experts. What has been said of New York City is true of all the principal cities of America, and a writer in the April number of the *Forum* describes the Irish bossing as 'a national ulcer,' to be thrown off sooner or later if American independence is ever to be anything more than a mere name. It is difficult for the Britisher, with his well-balanced municipal representation, to realize the full misfortune of all this. The trade union boss we know in George Square, in a mild and, as yet, harmless form, but we are lucky as citizens, inasmuch as the common sense of the electorate and good counsel have prevented any particular race, class, or interest from getting the upper hand of our civic affairs, although the attempt to establish the Boss is growing every year more determined. Let us be warned by the experience of America."

Thus much of party methods in the management and control of our elective system. It is the boast of our countrymen that the privilege of the elective franchise is universally enjoyed by every male citizen of the land; that in the free elections by the people of our rulers we have the safest guarantee for the maintenance of our rights and the integrity of our free institutions. What a travesty on a nation's autonomy and free institutions, when the most sacred rights of citizenship can be suspended, bought, sold, and exchanged, like second-hand wares in a public market. And yet the nation endorses this factional misrule as statesmanship, and the people boast of the liberty they enjoy under it. Would we might see ourselves as others see us.

CHAPTER X.

GERRYMANDERING.

ANOTHER scheme, equally reprehensible, which has been long in practice by the parties as a means of increasing their representatives in Congress, and in the Legislatures of the States, is called gerrymandering. This is a system of rearranging election districts so as to change majorities from one party to another. For example, there are in a certain State two Congressional districts, composed of three counties each. They are known perhaps as the Eighth and the Ninth District severally. The Eighth District has for some years given an average Democratic majority of five or six hundred, while the Ninth is Republican by a much larger majority. Now, the Legislature of this State having a Republican majority, they proceed to change the representation of the Eighth by taking from it a Democratic county, and putting in its stead a Republican county, at the same time placing the county removed from the Eighth into the Ninth District, thus leaving the Ninth still a Republican district, and making the Eighth also Republican, by which process one member of Congress is gained to the party. The same device is applicable to increase the party vote in the Legislature of the State. Republicans and Democrats seem to be equally zealous and unscrupulous in this nefarious work. It is often one of the earliest measures an incoming majority will adopt to make more sure what they have won and possess. That it is a gross fraud upon the entire people of the State need not be here asserted. It is especially a gross insult, gratuitously offered to those citizens who are moved about on a political chess-board in utter disregard of their wishes and of their rights as citizens.

Those opportunities and natural advantages which come to us in the course of trade or politics, are as much our possessions, as much our equitable interest that has accrued to us, as our honest earnings and our good name. To deny a competent voter, without sufficient reason, the right to vote for such persons as will represent him, Republican or Democrat, or by any device wrongfully to defeat his purpose in doing so, is practically to disfranchise him. These outrages are being constantly committed upon the rights of citizens by the parties whenever the opportunity offers. The people with their rights degraded and overridden are made pawns and puppets on the political gaming-table, and men who expect to be called statesmen, and have the prefix Hon. written with their names, sit down deliberately to this kind of computation and reasoning, for the purpose of defrauding their own neighbors and fellow-citizens.

CHAPTER XI.

GOVERNMENT PATRONAGE.

THE control and distribution of government patronage, State and national, is another device from which
political parties derive material aid in sustaining their
ascendency. This is the chief foundation and the
nursing mother from which the dominant party draws
its means of subsistence. It is the repository where the
bulk of their stock in trade is warehoused for future
use. It is a source of both honors and emoluments
in large supply, and from which all the rich plums of
political preferment are dispensed; hence it is the
cause of many bickerings and party feuds, and is a
source of constant peril to the party in power. This
patronage is immense, and is almost exclusively in
the hands of the President and the governors of the
several States in their jurisdiction. It is safe to say
that it is all used strictly on party lines and for the
reward of party services. In no part of the public
service is the maxim, "to the victor belong the spoils,"
more thoroughly adhered to or better illustrated. No
party can retain power, or any official, be he a governor of a State or President of the nation, maintain
the confidence and support of his party and ignore it.

The worst feature of this gross prostitution of the
honors and remunerations of the government service
is that it ignores the constitutional idea that in the

wisdom and discretion of the President and his constitutional advisers is vested the power to fill the various offices of the public service. While it is popularly supposed that he absolutely controls the entire
list of these preferments to place, it is really true that
he controls but a fraction of the assignments to office.
What is usually called executive or Presidential
patronage is by custom placed under the direction of
senators and representatives in Congress; and often
when a President has made an appointment that
proves to be a bad one, he will avail himself of this
usage in defence of criticism. As a rule these senators and representatives designate and recommend
all the persons who fill the offices of the State or district in which they reside. It is no uncommon occurrence to hear disappointed office-seekers at the
national capitol denounce this appointing power most
severely, and aver that, from the President and heads
of departments down to the superintendents of public
streets, all are liars and bribe-takers, and offenders in
many other ways against justice and fair dealing.
These persons have been promised, or suppose they
have been promised, an office under the government,
and in their own estimation have had every assurance
from head-quarters that they should obtain it; but
the pressure has been so great and imperative, and the
party necessity so urgent, that the President, or other
official controlling the matter, has felt compelled to
set aside the complaining candidate whom he had
given the greatest encouragement, if not an actual
promise, that his fond hopes should be realized.

Really the power behind all this official dignity, and which generally decides the fate of the candidates, is the primary and home influence of the party in the region where the candidate resides. There the contest for the place is mainly fought out and decided by the caucus bosses and the men who make up the party ticket in elections and carry the polling places by storm. They make their "demands," their "protests," and bring to bear their "pressure," if need be, upon the appointing power at Washington, and rarely fail of success. A senator may sometimes have a personal friend or political benefactor to reward, and he may practically ignore this local dictation; if so, he does it at his peril. The people, who are mere lookers-on in such a contest, are apt to suppose that the senator or representative is serenely canvassing the merits and demerits of the list of his friends and supporters in order to decide whom it is best to appoint, when, in fact, he is consulting and caucusing with the bosses and leaders of the party to ascertain whom he shall recommend for the place and not compromise his own position and prospects. The power behind the throne is greater than the throne, and doesn't care a button for it.

President Hayes at the opening of his administration gave the politicians distinct notice that he should not submit to their dictation in his appointments, but stand on his executive rights and discharge the responsibilities laid upon him without fear or favor. This announcement raised at once a bread-and-butter rebellion in the party. The writer well recollects with what displeasure the announcement was received in Washington, especially by the official class. It was a bold attempt to throw off the incubus of party dictation; but the party was stronger than their President, and they compelled him to modify his policy so as to conform to the usage of his predecessors. Thus the entire patronage of the government is used by the party in possession, to maintain its ascendency; and such persons are selected as recipients of it who will do the most for this object. It is commonly called "government pap," a commodity in the dispensing of which there is more bargain driving and knavery, more disappointment and heart-breaking, than is found in the gambling-hell or the stock exchange.

CHAPTER XII.

CLASS LEGISLATION.

CLASS legislation is another evil which is only made possible by the existence of political parties. There is much said in regard to the influence of corporations and combinations of various sorts upon political changes which are constantly occurring in the country; that these bodies control much of the current legislation, State and national, and that often the policy of a whole State is thus determined; and frequently the administration of the national government may be shaped at the dictation of a great railroad

system, which keeps its agents as members of legislative bodies in large numbers to do its bidding. It
is an open secret that the great trunk lines of this con-
tinent are in league with one another in defence of
legislation adverse to their interests, and that their
paid agents are constantly watching the course of
national and State legislation. The existence of
parties enables them successfully to do this. Indeed,
they are sought, and invited most cordially by the purveyors of these party organizations to an exchange of
favors. The party in power is always in need of
votes, for it must be continually fortifying against the
enemy. It cannot exist without this source of suste-
nance, and often it is in desperate circumstances, like
a debtor whose creditors have reached the limit of
forbearance. The administration is therefore always
in the market to exchange benefits with those who
can command votes. It will make vendable and put
upon the market all the available resources of the commonwealth, and they will be for sale or to let, or hy-
pothecated to the highest bidder, and in quantities to
suit the purchaser. If an individual or a corporation
has a large block of votes, and, as they say, "can de-
liver the goods," they will be quite sure to get what
they want. It is an open and well-known market for
all comers, and all classes will flock to it for investments. The result is an immense amount of class
legislation and the potent influence of combinations
in every branch of the government. There will be
whole communities bartering votes for local benefits,
the sale of indulgences to violators of law, the delay

or the defeat of justice in the courts, protection to il-
licit gains and to fraud and violence in multiplied
forms. All classes of associations who have votes to
barter for government aid flock to this national
market of reciprocal exchange, eager to interchange.
The great corporations, the merchants, the bankers,
manufacturers and miners, farmers and labor organizations, and the church even, making to itself friends
of the mammon of unrighteousness, bids with others
for a share in the spoils. Here is a great railroad
corporation that holds the balance of political power
in a State; it wants legislation to protect its holdings
and to enlarge the sphere of its gains; it wants lands,
or it is seeking to avoid its obligations to its creditors,
or to the people, and it packs a State Legislature or
has its lobby in Congress, and gains its desires. A
mining or manufacturing company who wants a
change in tariff laws; a sugar trust, a whiskey trust,
and an oil trust that want special privileges and a
chance to make more money; all the various trades
and occupations who by combining their strength
can give the party substantial support can change the
course of legislation and the flow of government
patronage in their favor from time to time, as their
interests require.

These people, the great mass of whom are otherwise
good citizens, excuse their share in this lobbying in-
famy by saying that there is no other way of obtaining
needed legislation or a fair share of government assistance; that it is a game free for all, and they pay
for what they get, etc. This is a chief source of

what is called class legislation in Congress and in the
State Legislatures. The general demoralization produced by these corrupt practices can scarcely be ap-
preciated by the public generally, so deeply are all
classes involved in it, and so popular has this method
of gambling in government futures and party promises become. The subject attracts but little serious
attention, and would be hushed to silence by the beneficiaries did not the opposing party persistently keep
the matter before the people for the purpose of dis-
crediting and defeating its opponent.

It is considered a good joke rather than a cause of
public indignation that a great railroad corporation
has obtained milions of acres of the public land without adequate compensation; and that a sugar trust or
a bond syndicate may adroitly pocket millions of the
public money as a result of a successful lobbying campaign at the seat of the national government.

I do not believe in much that is loosely said about
the direct use of money in purchasing the votes of
members of Congress and official persons at the capitol
of the nation. Wise men do not accept bribes, and
the politicians who are worth buying are too sharp to
engage in this dangerous traffic. But they will trade
for party support without losing their self-respect,
such as it is; and the man who has the largest available
"barrel" to party success can obtain almost any legislation that does not shock the sense of justice or de-
cency in the public mind.

CHAPTER XIII.

LOG-ROLLING.

ANOTHER kindred device for despoiling the United States treasury is the system of co-operative knavery known as "log-rolling," which is chiefly in use in Congress in passing appropriation bills. The early settlers of the wooded districts of this country were accustomed, in clearing up the forest lands for cultivation, to cut the heavy timber into logs of a convenient length and then invite their neighbors to what was called a "logging bee," which was a gathering of men and teams to put the logs into great piles suitable for burning. They called this joining of forces, changing work, as each man was liable to be called upon for a similar service in compensation for what he received. The politicians applied this principle in their tactics in use in obtaining the passage of appropriation bills in the national and State legislatures. From the soliciting and trading character of the work to be done in the passage of these bills, it came to be popularly called "log-rolling," from its co-operative character, or log-rolling a measure through Congress. The member who obtains a local appropriation for his constituents has acquired reputation and popular favor thereby, and holds a great card in his hand; it generally secures his renomination and otherwise lengthens his political career. There is, therefore, a universal desire on the part of members to draw a prize, great or small, in the log-rolling lottery of the River and Harbor Bill. In the preparation and passage of these bills, as from time to time reported in Congress, these tactics have been chiefly conspicuous and most successful. Each member who sees any possibility of getting an appropriation under this compact, for the improvement of any water-course or boat-landing in his district, is sure to bring his claim to the notice of the Appropriation Committee. It is there that the active log-rolling campaign begins. It is an active canvass on the part of each member for reciprocal assistance in securing what they individually desire. This is the ordinary form of solicitation: "Vote for me and I will vote for you; refuse, and we will combine and defeat the whole bill." After a great variety of combinations formed and dissolved, after an infinite amount of trading and huckstering, after much good-natured badinage and some exhibition of bad blood, the bill is "fixed up" and put upon its passage. So notorious has this gambling method of squandering the public money become, that Congress has by a general understanding limited these bills to the sum of twenty millions of dollars.

Such machinery in the hands of a billion dollar Congress without restraint or limit would soon bring the government to a condition of bankruptcy. It is not impossible that such a process of obtaining appropriations for what is in many cases a useless and profligate expenditure of money might be in use to a limited extent if there were no political parties in existence. They are only possible now from the fact that the general demoralization created by the partisan maladministration of the affairs of the nation gives license and immunity to such gambling with the people's money. When once the country is relieved of the presence of these organizations, the political atmosphere will clear up and such practices in legislative bodies will become well-nigh impossible.

CHAPTER XIV.

GOVERNMENT CONTRACTS.

THE letting of government contracts is another source of corruption and extravagant waste of public money. Nearly the entire annual expenditure of the government passes into the hands of a vast army of contractors, who furnish yearly supplies and material of various kinds needed to carry on the government. It is a notorious fact that the government pays always the highest price for everything it purchases, whether of products or labor; that what it buys is not of as good quality often as could be obtained by private enterprise for the same money; and that the service it employs is not up to the commercial standard of ability and general efficiency. It is a general rule, with few exceptions, that persons disburse the money of others more freely than they do their own. They will not economize expen-

7

diture as closely or be as diligent and faithful in
their labors as they are where themselves only are
benefited. This is especially true of expenditures
for the government. United States officials say
that the government requires the best of everything,
that all its supplies must be of superior quality, and
that it is able to pay liberally for what it requires.
They use a great deal of formality and red tape in
the contract system, without securing such result as
a private citizen would expect from the same expenditure of money. Hence the government is constantly the victim of fraud and collusion in the
quantity and quality of the commodities it purchases. The same is true of what it has to sell, be it
bonds, public lands, or valuable franchises. Everybody expects, in dealing with the government, to
buy at a low rate and to sell to it at a high rate.

This exceptional state of things is not difficult to
account for. It grows out of the fact that it does
not trade in a free market, but a market prescribed
by those who have an interest in high prices for government purchases and low prices for government
sales. The party in power always controls these
receipts and expenditures, and uniformly makes
them tributary to its support and aggrandizement.
Hence the contract system of the United States government is proverbially a field for fat contracts, paying jobs, and spoils generally. It is required by law
that these contracts be advertised and then let to
the highest bidder; this requirement is generally
complied with, but it always turns out, except in rare

instances, that the highest bidder is a member of the dominant party. Persons who are not in fellowship with that party, or who have no political backing, do not think it worth the time spent to bid on government contracts. It is a common saying that you must have plenty of pull to get a government contract.

The chief objection raised by many business men of experience in public affairs to the government ownership of railways, telegraph lines, and other great industries now owned and operated by the corporations of the country is that the government does everything in the most expensive way; that it pays the highest salaries, the greatest price for material and labor; that it cannot build a ship or erect a public building without there is a job in it, and more likely several of them, to add to the expenditure; that all such enterprise conducted by partisan appointees would open a still wider field for the corrupt practices already in vogue.

The United States government runs the Post-Office Department at an annual loss of several millions. With its seventy-five thousand postmasters, and half as many clerks and mail carriers, it has become a vast political machine which is used with partisan zeal and extravagance always in maintaining the ascendency of the dominant party. The bureau of Indian affairs and the department for the erection of public buildings through the country have for years had an unenviable reputation for jobbing and extravagance under the contract system.

We might in the same way refer to other branches of the public service were it needful to do so in order to convince any intelligent reader that our criticisms are just and our censures neither harsh nor improper. When we consider the low moral tone which prevails in all these partisan organizations and all the profligate and scandalous methods they employ, it would hardly seem prudent to give the spoilsmen and the political suspects of these combinations the power to choose from their own fraternities the men who are to hold or disburse the people's money. From the very purpose and composition of these trading coalitions, they cannot be patriotic or honest, and must legitimately and necessarily be untrustworthy and corrupt.

There are a few instances of this careless and wasteful method of expenditure under the direction of government officials which came within my own knowledge personally, which I will cite as abundantly corroborating what I have here averred in regard to their prodigality in the disbursement of public money.

The new Congressional Library at Washington stands on a square of ground near the Capitol building. It was thought necessary by those in charge of the construction of the new edifice that a fence should be placed around it to protect it from trespass during its erection. It had not been customary thus to encircle public buildings at the capital during progress of the work. The Capitol, the Treasury, and the War and Navy buildings were not thus enclosed while in process of construction. It was thought best, however, in this case to depart from the old customs by placing a tight board fence, six feet high, around the lot. This structure was made of cedar posts with first-class pine flooring, tongued and grooved, the whole work dressed and painted on both sides. This quite handsome and substantial environment cost the sum of eight thousand dollars. Such a large sum for a temporary fence, which would not sell for as many hundred dollars when taken down, was thought to be quite exorbitant by many people outside of official life. It was a subject of comment for a short time, but as there was nothing new about it, and the sum was small, it created more merriment than indignation at the capital. If you were to ask a citizen of Washington to explain to you how such extravagant prices were successfully levied upon the government for material and labor, he would likely respond, "Oh, there is a job in it, as there is in everything here."

Some years ago the United States government, with a view to increase the water supply in the city of Washington, undertook the construction of a tunnel from Georgetown over Rock Creek to the city. The legislation of Congress providing for its construction required that it should be built of stone, and be in all respects of first-class material and construction.

When it was about completed, as supposed, some employee upon the work, who had been discharged for cause, reported to a member of Congress, not of the Administration party, that there was gross neglect and fraud in the construction of the tunnel. These charges were soon verified by others acquainted with the facts, and soon a committee of Congress was appointed to investigate these rumors and inspect and report upon the work. This report revealed a state of things which astonished official circles even. The work had been done under the supervision of a government engineer of considerable reputation and ability. His assistants were United States engineers, and the whole force was abundantly equipped and supplied with everything required for the undertaking. Notwithstanding, the job was a scandal and a disgrace to all the responsible parties engaged in it, and had to be abandoned as not only unfit for the purpose for which it was designed, but as a structure unsafe to use and not worth reconstructing. The specifications required that all spaces in the excavations over the stone-work should be filled with stone laid in mortar. It was in evidence that there were spaces over the arch of the tunnel unfilled that a horse and cart might be driven into. The structure was abandoned for years.

The matter for a time was in very bad odor in Washington, but I do not think anybody was removed from office or punished for any fraud or neglect in the construction of the work.

I see that an effort is now being made by the citizens of Washington to have this unfortunate aqueduct overhauled and made to answer some useful purpose. I quote here an article of the *Washington Post* of March, 1897:

"The Board of Trade held a short session last evening at the Builders' Exchange hall, and adopted resolutions urging the passage of the bill for funds to complete the tunnel and reservoir. The following resolutions were unanimously adopted:

"WHEREAS, There have already been expended on the tunnel and reservoir nearly two and half million dollars, and the same is of no use in its present condition; and,

"WHEREAS, There is a pressing need of an increase in the water supply, especially on the higher grounds; and,

"WHEREAS, The Secretary of War and the chief engineers have approved of the plan reported by the commission of expert engineers for the completion of said work, and it is estimated that two years will be required for the completion of the same; therefore be it,

"*Resolved*, By the Board of Trade, that Congress be and is hereby respectfully and urgently requested to pass the pending bill at the present session for the completion of said work.

"*Resolved*, That the Secretary transmit a copy of the foregoing to the chairman of the Committee on Appropriations of the House and of the Senate."

Another very interesting item in this connection is the cost to the government of the official history of the war of the Rebellion. I quote from the Chicago *Record* a recent account of this large outlay for books, maps, charts, etc. The article is headed,—

"THE WORLD'S COSTLIEST BOOK.

"The most expensive book ever published in the world is the official history of the war of the Rebel-

lion, which is now being issued by the government
of the United States at a cost up to date of $2,334,-
328.   Of this amount, $1,184,291 has been paid for
printing and binding.   The remainder was expended
for salaries, rent, stationery and other contingent and
miscellaneous expenses, and for the purchase of
records from private individuals.   It will require at
least three years longer and an appropriation perhaps of $600,000 to complete the work, so that the
total cost will undoubtedly reach nearly $3,000,000.
It will consist of one hundred and twelve volumes,
including an index and an atlas, which contains one
hundred and seventy-eight plates and maps illus-
trating the important battles of the war, campaigns,
routes of march, plans of forts, and photographs of
interesting scenes, places, and persons.   Most of
these pictures are taken from photographs made by
the late M. B. Brady, of Washington.   Several years
ago the government purchased his stock of negatives
for a large sum of money.   Each volume will therefore cost an average of about $26,785, which proba-
bly exceeds that of any book that was ever issued.
Copies are sent free to public libraries, and one million three hundred and forty-seven thousand nine
hundred and ninety-nine have been so distributed.
The atlas costs $22.00, and the remainder of the
edition is sold at prices ranging from fifty cents to
ninety cents a volume.   There does not seem to be
a large popular demand, for only fifty-one thousand
one hundred and ninety-four copies have been sold
for only $30,154.   Thus it will be seen that the en-
tire proceeds from the sales thus far but slightly exceed the average cost of each of the one hundred
and twelve volumes.   The books can be obtained by
addressing the Secretary of War."

The Government Printing Office has been the
subject of a good deal of adverse criticism for many
years. It is a very large and expensive establishment, employing over a thousand men and women,
with a plant larger and more costly than anything
of the kind in the country. It is run on strictly
party lines, its employees being protégés and constituents of members of Congress generally. It is
said that the typographical unions, through their
allies in the national legislature, control the hours
and the price of labor in that department; that it
is a political and a trades union combination that
costs the government several millions annually.

It is claimed by Democrats that the Fifty-first
Congress, which was Republican, authorized the
expenditure of a billion dollars out of the national
treasury. This was stoutly denied by the Republicans, and they had their revenge in charging afterwards that the Fifty-third Congress, a Democratic
body, authorized an equal amount of expenditure,
which the Democrats also stoutly denied. Now, as
this is a partisan controversy and the arithmetic
methods of the parties are so thoroughly discredited,
we can only conjecture as to the actual truth in the
case. With a Congress so liberal in its appropriations, there is a great temptation on the part of government officials to make exorbitant demands upon
the treasury, and to be liberal and extravagant even,
in their disbursements for the public.

These cases that I have quoted are not altogether
exceptional and rare. Those who are familiar with

the want of prudence and economy in the construction of public works will corroborate from their own observations what I have here alleged in regard to the carelessness and wastefulness often exhibited in this branch of government expenditure.

The people of this country choose to govern it through party organizations, and to this end they have placed in their hands all the powers and resources of the nation. You cannot maintain parties without something for them to subsist upon. They are expensive institutions, and must have food and shelter, and, not content with this, for it is a poor compensation for the amount of hard and dirty work they do, they must have something for a rainy day and a good time generally, and the country ought liberally to support them so long as they employ them. To get their pay in the spoils of office, in government contracts, and from other like sources seems the most natural way, as every man should consistently get his pay out of his job as he does his work. It is in sad grace for the people to complain under all the circumstances.

CHAPTER XV.

CORRUPT USE OF THE UNITED STATES TERRITORIES.

ANOTHER striking example of the corrupt methods in use by the old political parties is the use for party ends made of the United States Territories by the dominant party during its lease of power. They are, from the time of their organization as civilized communities, to the day of their admission into the family of States, mere political appurtenances and conveniences of the dominant political faction at the seat of the government. They are deemed, taken, and held as perquisites and instruments of party power. As such they are used with little regard for the rights of those who inhabit them, or the wishes of the nation which is so largely responsible for their existence and well-doing. The principal offices of the Territories are filled at party dictation by the President at Washington, without consulting the wishes of the people residing within their limits, and often in opposition to their known views and feelings. In every Territory one or more political parties are organized and maintained, so that the party in power has its local organization on the ground, and its appointees have generally supervision and control of it.

The question of the admission of the Territory to the Union, which is always a pending one, is a mat-

ter of much consequence to its alma mater. If the
party needs the presence of two senators and an
increase of the membership of the lower house in
Congress, and the incoming State can give them this
party assistance, they will admit her to the Union,
though she may be entirely unfitted from the number and mixed character of her population to come
into the federal alliance on an equality with the
older States. Though she may lack the requisite
means to sustain the dignity and bear the burdens of
a State government, these considerations will inevitably yield to the paramount interests of the party.
On the other hand, though this prospective State can
furnish evidence that it has had for many years
every requisite for statehood, in population, wealth,
and general intelligence of her inhabitants, and that
the people are desirous of admission, and the interests of the Territory are suffering from its long
probation, these facts will be of no avail to them if
the dominant party has reason to fear that the representation from the State when admitted will diminish their party strength in Congress. Such a
territory will be kept out almost indefinitely unless
there is a change in its political complexion or a
change of majorities in Congress. Thus the material
prosperity and the final destiny of a great Territory
may be seriously affected by the caprice and tyranny
of a reigning political oligarchy. Here is a deliberate conspiracy to seize and hold the political
power of this Territory, solely to subserve party interests, an exercise of arbitrary power to restrain and
coerce it and to trade upon its rights.

Had we more space for the discussion of this branch of our subject, we might increase the number of specifications which sustain our charge of general corruption in the public service. As the New York chief of police said of his department, that it was honey-combed with corruption, so are we ready to affirm that the national and State governments of the country under the rule of the parties are to a shameful extent forums of knavery, injustice, and scandal. In all the departments at Washington there is embezzlement, depredation, jobbing, and inadequate service everywhere. The United States treasury, the General Post-Office, the Interior Department, the Departments of Justice and Agriculture, the War and Navy Departments, the Bureaus of Pensions and Patents, the Bureau of Engraving, and the Government Printing-Office, are all political machines, all made subservient to party behests, and all have been degraded to the use of venal politicians. They are organized, manned, and outfitted as much with reference to the profits and aggrandizement of party organization as a war-ship is outfitted for fighting the enemy. At every session of Congress some of them are under accusation and investigation for corrupt practices or abuse of power, for extravagance in expenditure, the delay of justice, and a partisan and selfish administration. They are a proverb throughout the nation, and were it not for the vigilance of the spies set upon them by the opposing party they would bankrupt the nation in a single Presidential term.

These parties seize upon the powers and perquisites of the government and administer its affairs simply for the spoils they can reap in the course of their tenancy. They have really no other interest in public affairs; hence they lay their corrupt and onerous tax levy upon every department and resource of the government, and spoliation and misrule is the general result.

Now, if these accusations of extravagance and corruption in the partisan management of public affairs are false, or exaggerated even, the writer must not be charged with malicious and libellous intentions, for his allegations are based upon and abundantly sustained by the admissions, investigations, and the repeated testimony of the organizations accused. The people are almost wholly indebted to these parties severally for the reliable knowledge they possess of their true character and the methods in vogue with them. The Democrats have for many years been loudly declaiming against the corruption and general incompetence of the Republican party, and are constantly producing accumulated evidence to prove their allegations. The Republicans, on the other hand, have been quite as often making similar charges against their antagonists, and have been quite as successful in producing evidence to sustain their counter-charges. Both these organizations are convicted of corruption and incompetence on the testimony of their own accomplices in crime. Six millions of Republican voters testify that the Democratic party is utterly depraved as an organization, and lacks the requisite mental and moral capacity to administer the affairs of the national government; that at several periods in the history of the nation it has brought the government to the verge of dissolution, and would soon ruin it if it could attain to uninterrupted power. About the same number of voting Democrats will give like testimony as to the character and general want of capacity of the Republican party. Everybody outside of these organizations would concur in these censures and share in the want of confidence they express.

Thus we have an almost unanimous manifestation of the state of public sentiment in regard to the vicious and depraved character of these associations. They are all engaged in a common conspiracy against the common weal; and when they turn State's evidence upon one another, they give us an opportunity to understand their true character. When a large majority of a man's neighbors are ready to testify that he is a rascal, you can impeach his veracity and general character in any court of the civilized world. The American press is constantly repeating these charges and denouncing these practices upon which we have dwelt, and if it is not malicious and mendacious in the last degree then its testimony must be taken as well-founded and of solemn import to the public. The spoils system in American politics is well known to fame. It has a reputation beyond seas, as a system better organized, more complete, efficient, and corrupt, than exists under any government under the sun.

CHAPTER XVI.

THE GRAND ARMY OF CONQUEST.

FEW persons have any definite conception of the magnitude and extent of these great political trades unions, the vast powers they exercise, and the immense resources they are able to command. At the last Presidential election the Democrats polled about six millions and a half of votes, and the Republicans upward of seven millions, altogether outnumbering the armies of the world. These several numbers constitute the membership of the two great parties who are known in their localities to be the avowed adherents and supporters of the section with whom they vote.

These federations are larger, each of them, than any other voluntary association in the United States. Either one of them has a larger membership than any Christian sect in the country. The Christian sects number about nine million members, all told, of every age and sex. The census of the political parties excludes women and children, as it does the great majority of the colored citizens of the Union. They are made up of citizens of the male sex who are of manly age and who possess the qualifications of electors.

The voting population of the country is its most efficient force for all the purposes of civilization. These are the persons who lead society everywhere, and shape the destinies of every nation. They are the most active, intelligent, and influential of the male population, and when they combine for any purpose and become distinctively a political class or a quasi corporation they are a most formidable and dangerous element in a free republic. These are the citizens in whom the Constitution has vested the sovereignty of the nation, and it is within the power of a small minority of them, if they selfishly and corruptly combine, to seize and hold the government for their own ambitious and mercenary ends as effectually as it might be done by force of arms.

The membership of this immense political propaganda is wide-spread throughout the length and breadth of the land, and each man of them is a partisan of more or less zeal and activity, and all of them are laborers in some way in doing service in the great work of making proselytes to the party faith and in sustaining the rule and prestige of the alliance. The most effective coworkers in these organizations are those who are the incumbents of office—and there are two hundred thousand of them on Uncle Sam's payroll—and those who are expectant of office. All these persons have a degree of training, discipline, and skill which makes them most efficient agents and bosses in the political field; for they have a personal interest in all the acquisitions made and the victories won by the party. Their bread and butter depends upon its perpetuity and its general success in carrying elections by the votes of the people.

It is estimated that there are several millions of

8

these persons in each of the great parties. The members of the dominant party constitute the ins, who are determined to retain their position, while the outs, a still larger and more determined host, are waiting and working for the succession. This army of workers finds occupation and does missionary work for the party in every portion of the country; "there is no land where their voice is not heard." Thus the party in ascendency has one or more efficient and well-paid agents in every township and hamlet in the land.

The party organization throughout, to the minutest detail, is most thorough and complete. There is the township committee in the rural districts, the ward clubs in the city, the county committee, the State organization, the national committee, and the party majority in Congress, which does more party work, distributes more partisan literature, furnishes more money, more positions for placemen, more fat jobs for its contractors, strikers, and lobbyists, than are derived from all other sources. The chief labors and anxieties of the average member of Congress arise out of his party relations, the service he is expected to perform to retain the party support. He is always a tired and overworked man from his excessive labors as a general politician and a purveyor of office for his hungry constitutents. The same is true of the ruling majority in each State Legislature; they supplement the work that the Congress is doing to sustain the common cause.

Each of the States has scores of officials distributed through its territory, who are doing a great deal of earnest work for the same purpose. In the remote and sparsely populated districts the town magistrate and constable, the supervisor and town clerk, the poor-master and the pound-master, the postmaster and the fence-viewer, the town collector and the school trustee are all active partisans. In the more populous districts these officials are multiplied to an astonishing extent, until they form a most active and efficient force in determining the politics of the State.

The national government has its representatives in the form of United States officials sent out by the dominant party. The judges of the United States District Courts and the United States district attorneys, the United States marshals and their deputies, clerks, bailiffs, detectives, etc., the collectors of customs and internal revenue officers, harbor masters and light-house keepers, pension and land commissioners, with the inevitable postmaster who does picket duty, day and night, for his party throughout his bailiwick, most zealously and industriously. These are supplemented by a movable corps of United States officials who do duty for the party as mounted men, who serve to keep up close communication between head-quarters and outlying posts. These are postal agents, inspectors and clerks, pension inspectors and detectives, revenue agents and detectives, agents of the Indian service, surveyors, engineers, and architects, with contractors and laborers on public works. This host of campaigners have all received their positions through partisan influence, and with a great majority of them their tenure of office will depend upon their increasing

activity and zeal in the party's interest. These placemen form in almost every township and ward in the
nation an advisory board and a working force, or both,
for the confederation to which they owe allegiance
and from which they derive support.

(In addition to this army of trained men, supervised
by the ablest politicians of the country, we have the
partisan press, the daily or weekly issues of which find
their way into every household, and constitutes perhaps the most powerful political agency in use by
these organizations. This powerful instrumentality
reaches all classes of society, the great mass of whose
members have a superstitious reverence for, if not a
belief in, whatever is alleged to be true in a newspaper. This partisan literature is so interlarded with
and served out with the current news of the day and
the state of trade, that thousands who feel no interest
whatever in politics or parties come, through the influence of what they at first read with indifference,
to be very decided and zealous partisans politically.
Through this agency the entire population may be
imbued with the partisan sentiment, and sustain or,
at least, apologize for all the party methods in vogue.

Through their silent influences the women and children of the country are in most cases quite as earnest
partisans as the opposite sex. Even those classes who
are supposed to have but a diminished interest in the
world's every-day affairs, such as soldiers, sailors,
clergymen, and aged and infirm men, are found uniformly to have their party preferences and alliances.

This mighty political force, under the control of

unscrupulous partisans, cannot be otherwise than a dangerous combination that should never possess to such an extent the confidence of the people or be trusted with the power it possesses.

These great associations, composed of millions of men, constitute a great army of occupation in possession of and quartered upon the country, scarcely excelled in numbers and efficiency by any military force ever mustered into service in any country. They outnumber all the armies of the world. Either of the two great parties can place more men in the field of their operations than were ever called into service in any war, ancient or modern. As a voluntary association they have a larger number of male citizens, a better organized and disciplined force, under their control than any other association of modern times. Some good citizens express fears that the Romish Church will gain undue ascendency in our politics; they are afraid of kingcraft and of the society of Jesuits, of the Freemasons and other secret societies, as endangering our liberties and free institutions; and yet they are members of these colossal organizations that have already usurped all the functions of government, State and national, that make all the laws and execute them, and rule the nation practically with despotic **power.**

CHAPTER XVII.

THE VAST POWERS THEY WIELD.

THE powers that such an organization may exercise through its right of possession are quite as extensive as are the number of agents it employs. It determines who shall be the chief elective officer and President of the republic. It selects a leading man of the party who is pledged to its interests and whose reputation as a politician and whose loyalty to the party is such that he can be trusted to administer the government in the interest of those who have placed him in power. They want a man who believes that public office is a public trust, and that he is the trustee of his party to distribute the spoils of office on that principle of Christian equity which declares that the laborer is worthy of his hire. They are very careful always in selecting their man, and whatever one's qualifications may be for this responsible office, he must give surety to his confederates and friends, without mental reservation, that he will be true to the time-honored doctrines and usages of the party, and that he will especially recognize the claims upon his gratitude made by those who have been chiefly instrumental in procuring his nomination and election. No man who is not a thorough partisan, and will be simply an agent and trustee of his party, can obtain a nomination even as President of the United States.

The governors of each of the States of the Union hold their offices by the same fiduciary tenure; they are all placemen, put in their positions by their auxiliaries to distribute among them the patronage of the State. The Congress and all the legislative bodies of the country are made up in the same way. They are composed of men who are party favorites at home, and who have been fortunate in securing the support of the local leaders in the district which they represent. This President is the chief executive officer of the government and commander-in-chief of the army and navy. He executes the laws which are not in conflict with the wishes of his party, and employs the military and naval force under his command.

Furthermore, the dominant party shapes all the legislation of the country, makes all such laws as the sentiment of the party demands, and executes and enforces such as are not in conflict with the interests of those who compose the organization. It appoints the judiciary of the nation, from a police justice in an inferior city to the Supreme Court of the United States. Every judicial officer must have the credentials of his party to his character as a devoted partisan who has seen much service in its ranks. His appointment is uniformly obtained through the efforts of the party leaders who recommend him as a member and favorite of the political household.

The same power dictates the financial policy of the country, coins all the money, controls the mints and its stock of gold and silver bullion, issues millions of bonds and other evidences of indebtedness and promises to pay of the people. It may create a public debt almost without limit, and then pay it or repudiate it. It uses the credit of the nation at its discretion, and often inflates or depresses it at the dictation and in the interest of its partisans. It dictates the foreign policy of the nation and executes treaties. It is in possession of the people's treasury and is the custodian of the public funds, the lord of the government exchequer, collects and holds all the revenues of the government, levies all taxes and the duties on all imports. It disburses three hundred and sixty millions annually of the people's money, the great bulk of which is paid to the members of the combination for services rendered or property purchased, for they are a trades union that seeks to deal exclusively with its own members where it is practicable to do so. It would be interesting to know how much of this vast sum finds its way to the pockets of those who are members of the party in power. All contracts are let if possible within the party circle and are taxed for party expenses. It employs only as its assistants and agents in administering the government those of its own guild. It determines the number it will employ and the compensation it will pay them. If any of them are defaulters or embezzlers their conduct will be investigated by a committee selected by party dictation and authority, and if they are prosecuted it will be very likely by a United States district attorney and tried by a judge and before a jury all of whom may be fellow Democrats or Republicans, as the case may occur.

The dominant party is the supreme power of the nation. It can make such laws as it chooses, and abolish all existing laws. It can abolish the Congress, the Supreme Court, and the Constitution itself, and change the present form of the federal government. They cannot change the organic law of the commonwealth, you reply, without a specific vote of the people. This vote they already control in majority. By various party devices these organizations have absorbed the individual sovereignity of the voter and exercise it as they choose, and always for party ends and party aggrandizement. The party in majority is stronger than the people, and can successfully defy them. This truth has been many times forcibly illustrated during the history of our government. While it continues in power it will be well-nigh absolute in the State.

These parties, absorbing and exercising as they do all the powers of government originally vested in the people, and standing in close relations with every moral and material interest of the nation, their influence is felt and is more or less potent and decisive in all the industries of the country and the occupation of every individual citizen. They have power to promote its highest and best interests, or they may, by unwise legislation, or by a corrupt and extravagant administration of its affairs, squander its revenue, or, in obedience to party dictation and a blind adherence to the doctrines of a party platform, reduce the revenues of the government to such an extent as to impair its credit and threaten it with insolvency.

It has come to be a matter of frequent occurrence
that the political action of these organizations are recognized as a disturbing force in financial and business
circles, for they have power to create the greatest
anxiety and depression in these spheres of activity.
They are able to produce financial panics and disaster to the business of the country in a multitude of
forms.   All these interests are in such a large measure under their control that by their incompetence,
their mistakes, or their deliberate gambling on the
public credit, it may not excite surprise that at any
time they may create a dangerous crisis in the business
interests of the country, involving losses to the public
from which they may not recover in many years.
War may be declared by party dictation, or from a
fancied necessity of saving the party consistency or
honor, where perhaps neither the honor nor the welfare of the nation requires it.   They may adopt a
foreign policy of such a character, or conduct the
foreign relations of the government in such a manner
as to embroil the country in a war with a friendly
nation even.   They can do this at their discretion,
inaugurate an unjust and disastrous war which they
may prolong almost indefinitely, or they may conclude it at any time with a dishonorable treaty of
peace.

Although these powerful party alliances have existed in this country for less than half a century, they
have during their brief history, at several important
junctures, involved the country in unnecessary war
and in wide-spread commercial disaster.   The present

depressed condition of trade, production, and the finances of the country, commencing some four years since, and from the influence of which the business of the country is but slowly recovering, I think is directly traceable to the factional strife which has always characterized the persistent efforts of these rival organizations for place and power.

The Presidential election of 1892 resulted in the defeat of the Republicans and the reinstatement of the Democrats in power, with Mr. Cleveland as President. It is generally conceded that the main issue at that election was the tariff, the Republicans advocating the doctrine of protection and the Democrats opposing any such revenue policy, denouncing it as unconstitutional and as a species of robbery of the consumers of foreign imports. Upon this issue the Republicans were beaten and went out of power. Immediately after the result was known the beaten party began to prophesy and croak disaster to the business interests of the country. Whether these words of ill omen arose out of a natural desire of the defeated party to see their antagonist unsuccessful in retaining its general popularity and a determination to destroy as far as possible the prestige of their victory and the public confidence in its future action, or whether it was a sincere conviction on the part of the Republicans that their rival was a free-trade organization who would evince by speedy legislation such hostilities to the tariff then in existence as to alarm the country and cause a suspension, at least, of some of the most flourishing industries of the nation, we cannot undertake to say. Under these circumstances, however, apprehension was not slow in taking possession of the public mind. The Republicans were predisposed, of course, to believe all they predicted as to the results of placing their old enemy in power; besides, this method of casting the political horoscope against an antagonist is recognized as quite admissible in party tactics. Current events of much significance contributed largely to sustain this contention of the losing party and aided them in obtaining credence for their portentous utterances. The Republican press and the party orators took up the same gloomy perspective of the affairs of the nation, so that before the first session of the new Congress, which had a large Democratic majority in the House of Representatives, there was a state of great anxiety and general distrust as to the action of that body on the question of the tariff.

When a great mass of persons, numbering five or six millions, become possessed with the idea that some great calamity or misfortune is reasonably to be apprehended in the near future, and they begin in concert to croak disaster and appeal loudly and earnestly to the people on any subject, they will very likely create a very profound impression, if not an actual panic, in the community where they reside. Such premonitions of evil are said to be contagious, so that the very air we breathe is a medium figuratively for the spread of such a popular apprehension. Such a formidable number of citizens are of themselves a body of public opinion whose warning will be heeded if there are either facts or current events to sustain their prophecies. The Republicans contended that the known views of the Democratic party on the questions of tariff and finance, together with the political complexion of the new Congress with its populist contingent, had created a feeling of general distrust and hesitation on the part of the capitalists and the business men of the country, which would manifest itself unmistakably in a disturbed condition of the money market, and in diminished production through every branch of industry and the consequent forced idleness and suffering of the laboring classes.

This feeling of apprehension that a financial storm was brewing caused all prudent people to take in sail and seek shelter until the future politically was more assured. It continued to grow until it became almost clamorous among all classes, until at length the party in power was appealed to by its friends and the great mass of citizens to forego all legislation upon the subject until the condition of the finances and the labor of the country became more settled. The appeal was not successful, though supported by large delegations of citizens visiting the seat of government for the special purpose of such remonstrance. Congress refused to grant the relief they sought, and refused in the midst of the greatest political, financial, and industrial crisis the country has ever witnessed. They continued through two sessions of that body, occupying a period of twenty months, to agitate changes in the tariff and the financial policy of the government, amidst the outcries and remonstrances of their constituents. In reply to these importunities they insisted that they had been placed in power on a tariff issue, that the Democratic platform pledged them to tariff reform, and to be consistent they must adhere to the platform and the time-honored policy of the party, against any remonstrances and at any cost to the country. They did persist in this adverse legislation until that Fifty-third Congress, ill-omened and memorable, expired by limitation.

The contest of these opposing parties over the measures in both houses has been the absorbing topic of the period through which it existed, so that it may be said that the severe political contest of the parties over the Presidential election of 1892 has been continued with all its original virulence and excitement for four years, resulting in a general paralysis of business throughout the Union. During this period the country has been lying prostrate and helpless beneath the feet of these giant organizations, whose Titanic struggles for supreme power have created an era in the history of the country, an era of bankruptcy, lawlessness, and political knight-errantry, which is scarcely excelled in any civilized country.

CHAPTER XVIII.

THEIR WAR RECORD.

I HAVE charged that the political parties of the period are made responsible in history for all the great wars in which we have been engaged for a century past. I do not mean simply that these wars have occurred while some political party was administering the government, but that in each case the cause, the crisis out of which they severally arose, was produced by the strife and selfish ambition of party leaders; and in some cases the war was declared and carried on for years for partisan purposes. This is noticeably true of the war of 1812. For ten years or more previous to this war our government was engaged in various controversies both with England and France in regard to our rights of commerce upon the high seas. The questions involved, as is always the case under like circumstances, became party questions. The then existing parties, the Republicans and the Federalists, took issue with one another on them and the measures proposed. Party spirit ran high, and in this controversy such a furor was raised against Great Britain that nothing would satisfy the Administration and its friends but a collision of arms with their ancient enemy of the mother country.

In June, 1812, the United States declared war

against England, Mr. Madison then being President, who, it is said, was opposed to the war. The Federalists were most heated and determined in their opposition to it, and were accused of in various ways giving aid and comfort to the enemy. Mr. Madison was a vascillating leader, and there were such party dissensions and party scandals as to impugn the patriotism of the American people and destroy the moral force of the republic in the controversy with the enemy. The war, though not disastrous to either side, has ever since been regarded as ill advised and fruitless of any great results commensurate with the expenditure of life and property in prosecuting it. It was a painful tragedy put on exhibition by the politicians and pursued to the last act to gratify their selfish ambition to retain place and power.

Mr. Rossiter Johnson in his history of the war of 1812, has this to say about some of the specific causes and circumstances under which it was inaugurated and carried on:

"Since the inauguration of President Jefferson the government had been in the hands of the Republicans, and all measures looking towards war with England were opposed by the party out of power,— the Federalists. The Federalists in Congress protested against the declaration of war, and this protest was repeated in every possible form by the Federal newspapers, by mass meetings, in numerous political pamphlets, and even in many pulpits. The opposition was especially strong in the New England States. The arguments of those who opposed the war were, that the country was not prepared for such a struggle, could not afford it, and would find it a hopeless undertaking; that the war policy had been forced upon Madison's administration by the Republican party in order to strengthen that party and keep it in power; that if we had cause for war with England we had cause for war with France also, and it was unreasonable to declare war against one of those powers and not against both. The last argument was the one the most vehemently urged, and the war party was denounced and censured, as making our government a tool of France. There was a certain amount of truth in each of these propositions. The country was very ill prepared for war at all, least of all with the most powerful of nations. Madison had probably been given to understand that unless he recommended a declaration of war he need not expect a renomination at the hands of his party. England by her sacrifice of life and property had gained absolutely nothing. She had not acquired an inch of territory or established a principle of international law, or purchased for herself any new privilege or secured any old one. It had caused a great deal of suffering and misery in this country by the derangement of business and destruction of property and loss of life. The war had cost the United States a hundred millions of dollars in money, and thirty thousand lives had been squandered, when with ordinary skill and care they might have been saved."

The Mexican War was the result of a long-cherished desire of the slave-holding South for the acquisition of more territory suited to slave labor. Mexican territory lying upon our borders was the coveted region. War was declared against Mexico in 1846. James K. Polk, of Tennessee, was elected President in 1844. Mr. Polk was a bigoted and well-trained partisan and a pronounced and zealous advocate for the extension of African slavery in the Territories of the United States. His cabinet, among whom were Buchanan, Secretary of State, and Marcy, Secretary of War, earnestly supported his views on this subject, and assisted in making it a party question with the Democratic constituency North and South.

The Whigs were the political rivals of the party in power, and opposed the war on the ground that it was sectional, a war to gratify the political ambition and cupidity of the South, as an unjust and causeless appeal to arms against a sister republic already overburdened with debt and the prey of contending factions within her borders. The South had for many years been the controlling section in the Democratic party. Under this influence the national government had from time to time, for years previous, attempted to purchase Mexican territory now known as Texas and California, but had never been successful. The colonization of Texas by citizens of the South was a scheme by the same parties in interest to secure by immigration what was denied them by purchase. The Southern people had at least three prime objects in view in the common movement. First, to increase the political power of the South; slavery had made them sectional and jealous of the rapid increase of the north in wealth and population. Second, they wanted to open fresh fields and pastures new for the dusky herds of slavery as well as homes for their owners; and third, to increase the price of slave property in the slave-breeding States. They publicly avowed these to be their objects in agitating and urging a contention with Mexico.

United States Senator Benton, of Missouri, who was strongly in favor of the acquisition of such territory, wrote a series of essays on the subject, and one of the reasons he assigned for the purchase of Texas was that five or six more slave-holding States might be thus added to the Union. In one of his calculations he estimates that nine more States as large as Kentucky might be formed within the limit of that province.

Said a Charleston journal upon the same subject: "It is an enterprise that could not fail to exercise an important and favorable influence upon the future destinies of the South, by increasing the votes of the slave-holding States in the United States Senate."

Judge Upshur, Secretary of State under President Tyler, said in the Virginia Convention, "If Texas should be obtained," which he strongly desired, "it would raise the price of slaves and be a great advantage to the slave-holders of the State."

Mr. Dodridge, in the same convention, said, "The acquisition of Texas will greatly enhance the value of the property in question."

Mr. Gholston, of the Virginia Legislature, said that he believed the acquisition of Texas would raise the price of the slaves fifty per cent.

The Mobile *Register* of that day advocated an increase of territory from Mexico for two reasons,—first, to equalize the South with the North; second, as a convenient and safe place, calculated from its peculiarly good soil and salubrious climate, for a slave population.

Mr. Mangum, senator from North Carolina, said, "There are now three millions of slaves penned up in the slave States, and they are an increasing population, increasing faster than the whites. And are the slaves always to be confined to their prison States?"

"We trust," said the Charleston *Patriot*, "that our Southern representatives will remember that this is a Southern war."

The *Courier*, of the same city, held this significant language: "Every battle fought in Mexico and every dollar spent there but insures the acquisition of territory and must widen the field of Southern enterprise and power for the future. And the final result will be to adjust the balance of power in the confederacy so as to give us the control over the operations of the government in all time to come."

These extracts, which might be multiplied almost indefinitely, are sufficient to show the trend of public opinion at the South, and the motive they had for a quarrel with Mexico which should result in open war. The slave-owners, having at their control the national government, under the administration of a President who was noted for his sectional zeal in promoting Southern interests, found little difficulty in using the whole force of the party in power in accomplishing their designs. The writer can well recollect that it was a very common thing during the period of hostillities to hear at the North the phrases used: "Mr. Polk's war;" "The slave-holder's war;" "The Democratic party's war." The South was not wholly responsible for it; there were Northern Democrats enough in the party to prevent its becoming the pliant agency which Southern politicians might use at their will; but they had long been accustomed to Southern dictation, and the crack of the party whip in hands accustomed to mastery brought them submissively into line when the votes were counted.

The Whigs very conclusively showed their want of sincerity in their loud denunciation of the war and the Administration, showing that political expediency was the motive of their opposition. On a vote upon a bill declaring that war existed by act of Mexico, and voting for fifty thousand volunteers and ten millions in money, they could muster only fourteen votes. It was an unjust and cruel war against a helpless and comparatively innocent people; and if public opinion in this country had not been brutalized and grossly depraved by the baleful influence of slavery upon it for generations, this record would never have stained the pages of American history.

Mexico had at that time a population of seven millions only, one million of whom were whites; while the majority of her population consisted of Indians, four millions; negroes, six thousand; and all other castes, two millions. She owed a national debt of eighty-five million dollars. Mr. Slidel, of Louisiana, who was sent by President Polk as minister to Mexico to further the designs of the government in the acquisition of territory, sent the following information to the State Department of the condition of the Mexican Republic at that time:

"The country, torn by conflicting factions, is in a state of perfect anarchy, its finances in a condition utterly desperate. I do not see where means can possibly be found to carry on the government. The annual expense of the army alone exceeds twenty-one million dollars, while the net revenue is not more than ten or twelve millions. While there is a prospect of war with the United States no capitalist will loan money, at any rate, however onerous. Every branch of the revenue is already pledged in advance. The troops must be paid or they will revolt."

As far back as 1829 the Mexican Congress passed a decree emancipating every slave in her territory. There was a strong anti-slavery sentiment in the country, and their chief opposition to any acquisition of any part of their domain by the United States was that it would become slave territory. It was, furthermore, regarded as only a beginning of the encroachments of the slave power. It was well understood that such was the object of our government in obtaining what it sought. This feeling was frequently exhibited in the official correspondence between the two governments before and during the war. Mr. Rejon, the Mexican Secretary, informed our minister, Mr. Shannon, on the 20th of October, 1844, that he "has orders to repel the protest now addressed to his government, and to declare that the

President of the United States is much mistaken, if he supposes Mexico capable of yielding to the menace which he, exceeding the powers given to him by the fundamental law of his nation, has directed against it." After commenting on the conduct of the United States, he concluded, "While one power is seeking more ground to stain by the slavery of an unfortunate branch of the human family, the other is endeavoring, by preserving what belongs to it, to diminish the surface which the former wants for this detestable traffic. Let the world now say which of the two has justice and reason on its side." It was manifestly a war of conquest in the interests of domestic slavery; and it was made possible and successful by the fact that the conspirators were organized as a national political party. Through that organization they did all their work; and had not the slave-holders of the South held a controlling influence in the party it never could have been used for such a purpose. The history of this war exhibits the immense power which these organizations possess and the base purposes for which they may be used as political agencies.

The war of the Rebellion furnishes another illustration, far more comprehensive and instructive, and quite as conclusive in the evidence it affords us that these political alliances constantly endanger the liberties of the people and menace often the national life. Previous to the election of Mr. Lincoln, in 1860, the Democratic party had been in power almost continuously for forty years. Recognizing the sectional feeling that has always existed in the slave-holding States, they very early made such concessions to it as secured to them, down to the present time, a large majority of the electoral votes of the South. They defended always, with much zeal and persistence, what they called the rights of the slave-holders under the Constitution; and during the thirty years of the heated and acrimonious discussion of slavery in the Northern States previous to the war they were champions and defenders of the South against all comers at home and abroad. Mr. Garrison used to denounce the party as the greatest pro-slavery organization of the age.

Mr. Lincoln, as the candidate of the Republican party, represented the anti-slavery sentiment of the North; and the slave-holders saw in that party an enemy to their cherished institution, too much in earnest to be appeased and too powerful to be contended with at close quarters on the political field, upon the issue whether the negro was a human being or a dehumanized monster and a chattel. They felt that they had no alternative but to secede from the Union in order to escape the Northern agitation and adverse legislation resulting in the abolition of slavery. Fully aware of the increasing sentiment against slavery in the North and forecasting their defeat at the national election, they resolved months previous to that event to go out of the Union should a Republican President be elected. Their hopes of successfully accomplishing this desperate scheme were based almost wholly upon the aid and comfort to be extended to them by the party in power, which had, at least, three or four months of legal existence left after its defeat. A few of the secession leaders believed that the country was ripe for a revolution against the abolitionists and their party, and that as the Democratic party in possession of the government was strong enough to hold it in spite of their rival's, they justified their acts on grounds of a necessity to save the Union. The same desperate class of politicians had succeeded in defiance of the North in annexing Texas and conquering Mexico through the instrumentality of the same party which, though now defeated in an election, had suffered no abatement in its numbers or its predatory spirit. They undoubtedly received abundant assurance of such aid. The history of the two parties shows that during the war they received such support from their Northern allies, not only on the floor of Congress, but throughout the Northern States.

Individual Democrats were exceedingly active and censorious. They were well-nigh frenzied in their rage towards the abolitionists, whom they described as treasonable instigators of the quarrel with the South, which now threatened the destruction of the nation. They denounced as unconstitutional and oppressive the efforts of loyal men to maintain the integrity of the Union at all hazzards. Public meetings were held throughout the North by such sympathizers with the Rebellion, for the purpose of producing a reaction in the public mind that should result in maintaining the status quo and saving both

slavery and the Union. The opinion was very generally expressed at the North by the opponents of
the incoming party that they could not prevent the
South from seceding, and that the North would not
enter upon a war of such magnitude and of such
doubtful results; that while the abolitionists, a
mere minority in the country, might sustain such a
war of coercion, the mass of the people had little
interest in the question beyond the addition of
further slave territory to the Union. I quote an
article from the Albany *Argus*, an old and leading
Democratic journal, which expressed the Democratic sentiment in regard to forcible resistance to
secession. The article was published in 1860, before
the election of Mr. Lincoln. It says,—

"Waiving, in what we have now to say, all questions about the right of secession, we believe, as a
matter of practical administration, neither Mr. Buchanan nor Mr. Lincoln will employ force against the
seceding States. If South Carolina, or any other
State, through a convention of her people, shall formally separate herself from the Union, probably both
the present and the next Executive will simply let
her alone and quietly allow all the functions of the
Federal government within her limits to be suspended.
Any other course would be madness, as it would at
once enlist all the Southern States in the controversy
and plunge the whole country into a civil war. The
first gun fired in the war of forcing a seceding State
back to her allegiance would probably prove the knell
to its final dismemberment. As a matter of policy
and wisdom, therefore, independent of the question
of right, we should deem resort to force most disastrous."

Mr. Buchanan and his cabinet as well were anxious and diligent in this patriotic work of saving at once the Union, the Democratic party, and the institution of slavery. The retiring President was a lifelong and earnest friend of the slave-holders of the South. His record was satisfactory to them, and they hoped everything from him in this emergency. In 1843, while he was in the United States Senate, he opposed the ratification of the treaty with Great Britain settling the northeast boundary, because it did not provide compensation for certain slaves liberated in the West Indies. He remarked, "All Christendom is leagued against the South upon the question of domestic slavery. They have no other allies to sustain their constitutional rights except the Democracy of the North. In my own State we inscribe upon our party banners, 'Hostility to abolitions.' It is there one of the cardinal principles of the Democratic party." In his last message to Congress he said, "Has the Constitution delegated to Congress power to coerce into submission a State which is attempting to withdraw, or has actually withdrawn, from the Confederacy? If answered in the affirmative it must be on the principle that the power has been conferred upon Congress to declare and make war against a State. After much serious reflection, I have arrived at the conclusion that no such power has been delegated to Congress, or to any other department of the Federal government." He recommended as a settlement of the differences between the North and the South an explanatory amendment of the Constitution, providing, first, express recognition of the right of property in slaves in the States where it now exists, or may hereafter exist. Second, the duty of protecting this right in all the common territories throughout their territorial existence. Third, a recognition of the right of the master to his slave who has escaped from him to another State, to be restored, delivered up to him. Fourth, that the validity of the fugitive slave law, together with a declaration that all State laws impairing or defeating this right, are violations of the Constitution and are consequently null and void.

This doctrine was sustained by his Attorney-General, Judge Black, in an elaborate opinion. He said, "If it be true that war cannot be declared, nor a system of general hostilities be carried on by the central government against a State, then it seems to follow that an attempt to do so would be *ipso facto* an expulsion of such State from the Union; being treated as an alien and an enemy she would be compelled to act accordingly. And if Congress shall break up the present Union by unconstitutionally putting strife, enmity, and armed hostility between the different sections of the country instead of the 'domestic tranquillity' which the Constitution was meant to insure, will not all the States be absolved from their federal obligations? Is any portion of the people bound to contribute their money or their blood to carry on a contest like that?"

This was Democratic doctrine as announced from the highest authority of the party. And it was generally accepted by the rank and file and acted upon most diligently throughout the war. This was the kind of aid and comfort, the moral support, which the secessionists anticipated and chiefly depended upon before going out of the Union. If their Northern friends did not prevent the inauguration of Mr. Lincoln by a general defection and rising of the people aided by the government, still in the hands friendly to their interests, they, at least, hoped that they would succeed in so dividing and distracting the Northern sentiment to a degree that no effective resistance would be made against their traitorous movement. That these hopes were defeated was not due to any zeal or determined effort on the part of their Northern friends and allies in and out of Congress.

The war of the Rebellion was a war among partisans. It was instigated by party intrigue and carried forward as a distinct issue between the two parties to the end. Had there been no Democratic party to countenance the secession movement early in its history, it never would have assumed a dangerous aspect. An occasional threat on the floor of Congress and in the partisan newspapers at the South would have embodied the measure of its constituent strength and general influence. It was an infant enterprise that came to be formidable by the lapse of time and good nursing. Had there been no parties at all, there would have been no rebellion.

To the charge that the Democrats are responsible for the war they enter an indignant denial and earnestly assert that the Republicans were the instigators of the quarrel between the sections, by unwarranted attacks upon the domestic institutions of the South, by threatening to destroy twelve hundred millions of dollars' worth of property in slaves (Henry Clay's estimate), and to let loose upon them their emancipated negroes, to overrun and impoverish the country; that to escape these calamities, which were imminent and overwhelming, they seceded from the Union as their only refuge. Now, we do not propose to act as umpire in this contest, but to let these parties settle the question as to which of them did the most to involve the country in a four years' war over a question that should have been settled elsewhere without the shedding of blood. Very certain it is, had there been no political parties to manage and make capital out of the case, there would have been no civil war about it. Had there been no Democratic party the South would not have seceded. Had there been no Republican party they would have remained undisturbed in the Union.

These disagreements which often occur between sections and nationalities not unfrequently lead to open hostilities and a state of war where they have not been conducted in a spirit of toleration, of justice, and mutual concession. Where there is party bias and party interests to be subserved, questions in controversy are not likely to be treated with judicial fairness and amicably settled. Whenever in this country there are conflicting claims or matters in dispute between ourselves and a foreign nation, the controversy is carried forward by direction of the President through the Secretary of State. Whenever the Administration indicates its views and its line of policy in regard to the differences in question, immediately and inevitably the opposing political party announces its dissent and its earnest protest against the views officially declared. Its press immediately takes up the question adversely to the government, and the whole force and influence of the opposing party is relentlessly used to embarrass the Administration and precipitate a crisis that shall disgrace the party in power, or make it responsible for a causeless and unpopular war. It seizes the opportunity in such a critical period of our foreign relations to make political capital out of a national emergency. By impeaching the motives of the government and casting discredit upon the evidence by which it seeks to sustain its side of the controversy, they give aid and comfort to the enemy in the dispute, encouraging them to persist in their unreasonable demands. Meantime, the party in power, to be consistent with its contentions and not bring disgrace upon itself and the country by yielding to unjust exactments, embroils the nation in a needless and expensive war.

In the history of parties throughout the civilized world, it has been charged, and truly, I believe, that in certain nationalities they have been guilty of the monstrous crime of inciting internal revolution and foreign war, as a means of securing political power or of retaining it under a waning support.

CHAPTER XIX.

UNAUTHORIZED AND IRRESPONSIBLE.

THESE federations, as it is said of corporations, have no souls; they have not even a respectable moral code. A work on the ethics of American politics would be a literary curiosity. What compensation do they give the public for these high privileges? What guarantee do they tender that these great trusts shall be faithfully executed? It would seem that persons, parties, corporations, or combinations of any such description, wielding powers so vast and diverse in their nature for the good or evil of society, should be in a high degree responsible—yes, in the highest degree responsible—for their acts; and should, futhermore, possess a general reputation for integrity and capacity that cannot be impeached and is quite above suspicion. Who vouches for the honor and fidelity of these organizations? Who will be surety for their loyalty and incorruptibility in the discharge of the trust assigned them by the people? Is there any corporation or syndicate in this country or in Europe that would at any price go bail or underwrite for the rectitude and trustworthiness of any of our political factions? As party organizations they are wholly irresponsible and are a law unto themselves, whether they have been placed in power by the votes of the people or are waiting and laboring in expectancy of what they may never attain. They claim this immunity from all responsibility by prescriptive right. They are in no way amenable to law.

Other voluntary associations, engaged in occupations for profit, are answerable to the laws of the land. Corporations must have charters which may be amended or revoked by lawful authority. They pay taxes and report their incomes and the profit and extent of their business to those who administer the laws. They are chargeable with certain duties and are restrained from the commission of acts in derogation of the rights of the public. Partnerships, trusts, lotteries, and joint stock companies, together with all communities, fraternities, brotherhoods, etc., are answerable to the law, and liable for their acts in the courts of justice when charged with violation of law and the rights of society. No court has jurisdiction of a political party, no grand jury can indict them, and no public officer can prosecute them for any offence. They can not be judicially impeached or enjoined; they are not legally liable on their contracts; they cannot be sued, arrested, or served with legal process, whatever their offences may be. Their crimes are not punishable, even though they may exceed in magnitude those of all other criminals. They have no credit, and their promises to pay are of no commercial value. It is a most common thing for them to repudiate their most sacred obligations and deny their express promises. Though large sums of money come into their hands and they spend it lavishly to promote the interests and general prosperity of the association, you cannot enforce the collection of a debt for goods sold and delivered, or a claim for damages to persons or property.

How would you proceed to collect the people's bill for damages against the political parties in and out of power during the past four years? They are above the law and above the Constitution, and can violate either of them with impunity. There is no law, human or divine, that can restrain or punish a political party, whatever its acts may be. They can persist in a course of maladministration which may bring disaster to the country and suffering and privation into every family in the land, and the people will be absolutely without remedy. They cannot displace them and employ a better service, for they have a fixed tenure of possession which must first expire. They are beyond the control of public opinion and can defy it indefinitely. The whole country may be weary of them and unanimously condemn and repudiate them, but they never resign. A public expression of want of confidence is of little significance in this country, and politicians never relinquish office because they are censured or admonished. We have no alternative but revolution or to patiently endure the wrongs inflicted until their term expires by limitation. There is no other body known to civilized society which enjoys such multiplied privileges and immunities, and we may add, no other association so grossly abuses its special indulgences or betrays so ungratefully the confidence of the people.

Suppose an association of bankers and brokers, composed of persons from different parts of the country, should, by the same party devices as are now in use in shaping public policy, obtain such legislation from Congress as would give them the possession and control of the United States Treasury Department as agents of the government, authorizing the association to fill all the offices existing in the Department at Washington and elsewhere, giving it possession of the paper money factory at the capital, called the Bureau of Engraving and Printing, with the power to employ it for the issue of money at their discretion. Suppose they had like authority and possession of the government mints and sub-treasuries elsewhere, together with the custom-houses over the country, and all other branches of the service, so that it could collect all the revenue, coin all the gold and silver, issue at pleasure all the notes and bonds of the government, and determine the whole financial policy of the nation, administering the affairs of the national treasury with the same freedom and absolute control which the party in power at present exercises. Let us further suppose that this association was altogether a voluntary affair, whose reputation for business capacity and general integrity was very generally questioned; that it gives no bonds for the faithful discharge of its duties beyond the individual bonds of some of its employees; that there was no legal restraint upon its authority or its acts, and the good faith and integrity of its administration was dependent upon the sentiment of honor and fair-dealing which prevailed among the members of the association. Could any

citizen of this country not personally interested in the
spoils of such a scheme be induced to sanction it?
And yet the parallel is not overdrawn.

If these are proper bodies to be intrusted with the
plenary powers which they wield, if the lives and
property of the people and the destinies of the nation
are to be submitted to this species of vicarious, irresponsible authority, make it amenable to law, the
first requisite to citizenship. Make them give bond
for good behavior and a safe and honest administration of the vast interests intrusted to their care. If
we want to farm out the national government every
four years to some voluntary association, let us look
for a reputable and responsible tenant. The old occupants, these mesne lords and their retainers, have
long been guilty of waste and bad management of
the people's inheritance. The nation is weary of
them, and though their stewardship is discredited
and their general character publicly impeached, they
continue by various devices to hold on and hold over.
Let the nation call these organizations to a strict ac-
counting, issue its *quo warranto* against them to
show by what authority they use the powers with
which they are intrusted for their own advantage
and profit and not primarily for the welfare of the
public. They are in possession, by permission of the
people, of vast powers, which they abuse, and of im-
·mense sums of money, which they squander. They
are charged by common fame with corrupting the
public service and demoralizing the people; let them
show that these charges are not true, or, if true, that

their services are necessary to the people, who receive adequate compensation in their diligent administration of the affairs of the nation for all the losses and dishonor the nation suffers through them. Let us have a contract suited to such grants of power and patronage, some guarantee that the country shall not be brought to the verge of bankruptcy every few years or be involved in needless and dishonorable wars; some assurance that the national credit shall not be destroyed, its industries harassed and crippled by conflicting legislation; that its civil service shall not become a trading mart in the interests of partisan jobbers and political Simonists.

If the people wish to be governed by a joint stock company, by some powerful and wealthy corporation, or by some respectable religious sect, I have little doubt that they could obtain better service with less risk and smaller expenditure of money than we are now getting at the cost of a million dollars per day. What is it now but a leasehold to a thriftless and wasteful tenant, who taxes to the utmost the patience and the industry of the people to keep the estate in repair?

Suppose either of those respectable bodies, the society of Freemasons or the Independent Order of Odd Fellows, should attempt to capture the government, ostensibly to promote some needful reforms in the interests of the public, but really for the profit and aggrandizement of the Order; or suppose some religious sect, Catholic or Protestant, should commence an intrigue and a campaign for the same

purpose, setting forth as good grounds for such a
demonstration the general corruption and the incompetency of the present party, and the universal distrust and want of confidence in them, manifested by
the people; that the people have confidence in the
church and its clergy; that the ecclesiastics of the
church are quite superior to the present race of politicians in morals and manners and general ability;
that the church, assured of divine assistance, which
the politicians neither seek nor obtain, would be enabled to administer the government for the temporal
and spiritual welfare of all the people,—what a cry
of indignation would the publication of such a mani-
festo create in every hamlet in the country, a derisive
yet an apprehensive cry of disapproval! What
changes would be rung upon the words priestcraft,
popery, church and state!

No such attempt would be openly sustained by
any Christian denomination, and no such movement
could succeed in this country. The people would
not trust any other organization, religious or secular,
with the powers they so blindly bestow upon party
organizations to which they and their fathers have
for centuries given their allegiance. And yet one
may inquire, why not? If we are to put the political
power of the country into the hands of some coalition or league to do the necessary work of carrying
on the government, and take our chances as to their
honesty and general capacity, the amount they may
steal, and the general demoralization they may
create, why not try by popular vote to elect some

organization of known responsibility and general character to assume this patriotic task?

It could scarcely be a policy more unwise, should the majority of the people vote for it, to let the Methodist Church administer the United States government for the glory of God and the salvation of souls, with "incidental protection" to church interests, than to give the Republican party a *carte blanche* to run the government for four years for the glory of the party and the good of the politicians and bosses who control it. A United States Senate made up of bishops of the church, and the lower house of good, honest class-leaders of the denomination, excluding all persons notoriously immoral, all third-rate lawyers, and persons who have been charged with crime, would command a measure of respect and confidence which these bodies do not usually enjoy. You would, at least, have a Congress that would in many respects be a marked improvement on the Fifty-third, of savory memory. There would be fewer brawls and pugilistic contests, and perhaps less waste of valuable time, and better attention to the legitimate business of that body.

We perhaps might make a very advantageous bargain with Leo XIII., the present head of the Romish Church, to enter upon the arduous and responsible task of governing the American commonwealth. He has always manifested great interest in the temporal and spiritual welfare of the American people. The papacy has, furthermore, had large experience in the exercise of temporal power and in the government of foreign states. There has hardly been a civilized state in Europe for centuries that has not submitted to his counsel, and been largely controlled by his infallible judgment in temporal and spiritual affairs. No Christian sect has manifested more interest and zeal in civil affairs, or as much, perhaps, as the Romish Church. Its members have always manifested an earnest determination to support the institutions of this country, and to assist in person, as far as possible, in the execution of the laws and in the maintenance of order in the several communities, notably in the large cities like New York and Chicago, where it would be impossible to fill the municipal offices satisfactorily to the government if there did not happen to be a large number of Irish Catholics to volunteer their services to the country of their adoption.

Some sectarian prejudice might be created by such an attempt to transfer the political power of the country from a political to a religious hierarchy, but all sensible citizens would hardly fail to see that their could be in the case no essential difference between a Pope elected by a college of Cardinals of the Church and a partisan President chosen by a college of electors of his own party. If any of the associations known to modern society should attempt the possession or the exercise of such tremendous powers, though they might be supported by a majority of the people, every sensible and patriotic man would oppose such a movement as dangerous and impolitic. Every citizen with any experience in the administration of civil government, or ordinary knowledge of the general qualifications of popular and miscellaneous societies to manage important public affairs, would regard such a suggestion as too absurd for any serious consideration. What else is a political party but a voluntary association without prerogative or authority superior to other bodies of citizens? They have no official recognition as government agents, neither can they obtain any such endorsement or voucher of authority from such a source. No citizen is supposed to act as a Republican, a Democrat, or a Populist; the voter is a citizen and not a party. No voluntary association of citizens can force themselves upon the people and by any devices be recognized as exercising the sovereignty vested in the people. We speak of them as though they were vested by the Constitution with the right to represent the people, and with a degree of independent sovereignty in the administration of public affairs. We speak of them as the party in power, as being in such a case the government *de facto* and *de jure*. They have no ruling power, are not clothed with powerful authority. They have assumed an importance that is unreal, and have obtained a prestige to which they are not entitled. They are the instruments merely of the people, and not their political guardians. They are the creatures of the hour, of the popular will, and the hands that use them to-day may vengefully destroy them to-morrow.

CHAPTER XX.

PARTISAN CONTROVERSY AN ENDLESS CHAIN.

WHILE these organizations, as political agencies, are morally defective, and thus in a marked degree unfitted to discharge the responsibilities they assume, they are equally incapable of any impartial and dispassionate consideration of those questions which make up the issues between the great parties of this country. A partisan is generally a person who is biassed in his opinions and one-sided in his views of all questions affecting the practice or the creed of his party. The sect or party which has announced to the world a creed or a platform of opinions, and challenged a public discussion of its merits, has thus far prejudged and decided the questions in controversy, and is itself incapable of any but a partial and one-sided treatment of them. Its members have a fixed belief to which they are publicly committed, and have a vital interest in sustaining their opinions, on which the cause they advocate depends. Party spirit has produced in them obliquity of judgment, which disqualifies them more or less as public teachers and leaders of their particular class or section.

A partisan has, in sustaining his contention, a pride and a sense of loyalty to his guild; and he well knows that the public would lose confidence in it and its declarations, and that his rivals would be ready to sound a note of triumph, if he should admit but a single error in his political platform. He must sustain the traditions and doctrines of his party and the currrent methods of propagating its opinions and maintaining its ascendency at all hazards. It is the boast of the old political parties that their opinions on public questions are time-honored and venerable in years, that they have descended to them from the fathers of the republic, and have the sanction of the wisest and purest patriots of that early period in the history of the government. They quote Jefferson and Jackson and Adams and Hamilton as statesmen of the past who held the opinions they now put forth; and the fact that these distinguished men in our political history advocated certain public measures gives them a wonderful, and many people are inclined to think an undue, prestige and influence among the politicians and those whom they lead. The teachings of Moses and the Prophets in their influence upon the Christian sentiment of the country are scarcely more potent and inspiring than the political dogmas of these eminent men. Undoubtedly the average politician has a greater reverence for the latter than for the former high authority. That it exerts a more potent influence over his life will be generally conceded. The traditions of a political party are as sacred and binding upon its members as those of the church. They hold that order and consistency require that there should be no change in the principles or policy of the organization. The doctrines of Jackson, Jefferson, Clay, and Lincoln are precedents, and each party boasts of its uniform adherence to them. There can be no genuine progress in such organizations. They are repressive rather of advancing civilization and of all reforms in civil government. Their declarations and platforms abound in much cheap rhetoric about progress and reform, while their history shows that they are afflicted with a chronic conservatism, an inherent malady running in the blood, from which political combinations never recover. They have boxed the political compass; within its thirty-two points there is nothing new for them to learn, and they will never have anything new or original to teach the public.

We judge that there is a growing belief among intelligent persons outside of party organizations that the grave questions involved in the administration of civil governments should be discussed on their merits, rather than decided on the expressed opinions of statesmen of the past century. In the evolution of society great changes have occurred in the forces and factors which made up the political situation fifty years ago. These wonderful changes in our population, in the earnings and industries of the nation, and in the general character of our people will suggest to the reader whether the laws governing a modern commonwealth should be like those of the Medes and Persians, unchangeable. When any question of public interest is thrown into the maelstrom of political discussion and becomes a party issue, there is an end of all hope of a satisfactory solution of it by the people. It becomes a partisan controversy, and nobody expects that there will be any change of opinion on either side of the contest. The public mind becomes so benumbed and confused by the contentions of the politicians and the party press, reiterating from year to year the same stale lamentations as to the political condition of the country, and fulminating their indignation against one another, that the great mass of citizens are unable to vote intelligently upon such party issues. They inaugurate campaigns of education, loading the mails with partisan literature for free distribution, while at certain seasons of the year the land is vocal with the prophetic eloquence of the itinerant stump speaker and the village wrangler; but all these varied efforts serve only to increase that state of political obfuscation into which the average voter seems hopelessly to have fallen.

Mr. Dickens, in his character of Stephen Blackpool, has described this state of political quandary in which an honest citizen is sometimes involved when he wishes to cast his vote in the best interest of society. Stephen was a power loom weaver in a great cotton-mill in England. He was a man of moderate abilities, but capable and honest in the discharge of his duties as an employee, and was quite respected for these qualities by those who knew him. Humble citizen as he was, all the agitators of opinion had use for him. He was therefore beset at every turn by the trades unions and politicians and the agents and bosses of the employers of Coketown, who sought to capture

for their own profit whatever he could command of
votes or influence among his fellows. To this purpose they plied and overwhelmed him with rival arguments and conflicting statements of theory and fact,
which resulted in a sort of collapse and utter confusion of his reasoning faculties. He finally sums up
and dismisses the whole controversy in these words:
"'Tis a muddle and that's aw. Alwus a muddle.
There is where I stick. I come to the muddle many
times and agen, and I never get beyond it."

Partisans never have settled and never can settle
any matter in controversy between them. They have
fixed ideas of public affairs, and are so biassed and
pledged by time-worn traditions and party platforms
that they are incapable of adapting themselves to the
changing conditions of society. The history of the
political parties of this country abundantly sustains
these assertions. For half a century or more they
have been discussing, pro and con, the tariff, the currency, and other collateral questions which enter into
the administration of civil government. These subjects to-day are as seriously and earnestly in controversy by these rival organizations as at any period in
our history, showing that they are quite incapable of
establishing anything like a permanent policy by
which the country may be governed. The political
embroglio which they created half a century ago
promises to be permanent so long as this war of words
shall last.

It is in vain that national elections are held where
these questions are distinctly in issue and where the

parties go to the country on such issues joined. The beaten party, instead of accepting the result as the verdict of the people, and as conclusive as a repudiation of their political theories and measures, at once commence a fresh campaign to set this verdict aside. Thus in the political field we have an endless strife, one that will never terminate while we furnish prizes to be won by the contestants. The truth is, the political partisans do not want these questions settled in the public mind; the agitation of them is their stock in trade, their only capital on which they do business. They must have issues upon which they can appeal to the people; they must have a public grievance, a pending calamity, or some immediate threat or menace against the liberties and happiness of the people and the security of our institutions. This campaign material, by a sort of mutual exchange, is furnished by the parties themselves, the one to the other. Each organization has only to draw upon the platform the general character and history of its antagonist to make a case that is sure to alarm and stir to action a large number of the voting population. The country has no need of a saviour, a power to protect it, unless some danger is imminent. Each party, therefore, must keep in stock the indubitable evidence of combinations and conspiracies of corrupt and incompetent persons to seize the reins of government and use its power solely to their own advantage. They must have a standing quarrel and difference of views in all public questions with rival organizations, and be able to show that their antagonists are bent upon ruining the country and that they themselves hold the key to the situation and have come to the rescue simply from patriotic motives. They thus use one another as spectres and bugaboos, playing upon the fears of the people and dividing them into factions who will be subservient to their wishes.

These political differences might easily be settled if the contestants were in earnest for harmony of views and action among the people on political topics. A non-partisan Congress, having only the welfare of the nation to legislate for, would soon compromise and harmonize all these adverse interests, to the great relief and satisfaction of the nation. But this would imply the abandonment of party organization and an end of the spoils system.

Current events sometimes narrow the issues between the parties to the extent that sensible people begin to wonder what they can find to quarrel about, why they don't come together, bury the hatchet, and give the country a rest. On the contrary, at such a time the politicians always hasten to widen such a closing breach by some new declaration or device. Each party must necessarily oppose every measure adopted by its antagonist, and any concession is regarded as a confession of weakness in political warfare. Thus there is a perpetual deadlock of platforms, and an endless controversy upon dead and unnecessary issues; and this fight of scurrility and detraction is what in this country is comprehensively called politics,—the synonyme of knavery and corruption and the avoidance of honest men.

It is unfortunate that the great anxiety and uncertainty in which the political sphere is involved in consequence of this state of agitation is so largely shared by the business and industrial world. The party politicians have taught the people for generations that the prosperity of the country depends upon their action while in power, and that the destinies of the republic are completely in their hands. The great mass of the people quite credit it, too, and sustain their assumptions; hence the action of these organizations, legislative and executive, have come to exert a marked influence upon the business interests of the country and upon its general prosperity. Trade and commerce, and all the industries of the nation frequently wait upon the results of an election. The business of the country is at times almost suspended, waiting to know which of the great parties will be in the ascendency for the coming four years, and what will be the policy of the victors. This, notwithstanding platforms and promises, may be a very uncertain question to determine. You will often hear men say, in view of making investments, or starting some new enterprise, that they must postpone it until after election, or until they see what Congress is going to do.

So long as the political situation is controlled by the parties, the business of the country must be unstable and insecure, must lack that uniformity and promise of permanence so necessary to inspire confidence and enterprise in those who do the business of the world. We have heard it constantly repeated by all classes of citizens during the depression of the

past few years, that there seems to be nothing wanting
to bring a return of prosperity to business interests
but the return of confidence. It is said there is
money in abundance, and that it can be had at a low
rate of interest; that there is a large stock of raw material and of manufactured goods, and a large supply
of the products of the soil and the necessaries of life;
that there are men enough and women enough to perform all the labor of the country and handle its business. There is an over-supply of everything we need,
yet labor is idle and trade and commerce languish,
capital is reluctant and business men are waiting and
hedging, and everybody is living from hand to mouth.

In such a condition of things all eyes are turned
to the action of the political parties. A canvas involving a change of national administration is a matter of supreme moment to the people, for from the
results they can ascertain what will be the policy of
the government in relation to vital questions which
exert so much influence on the general prosperity of
the country. They know that for the next four years
there will be something like stability and uniformity
in the course of trade and production; that it will last,
in spite of the opposing party's efforts to obstruct and
decry it, for four years more or less, before another
material change can be forced upon the country.

A government so impeded and helpless through the
strife of political factions who have obtained control
of its sovereign power and patronage that it can give
to its people and to the world with whom it trades no
assurance in regard to its future policy, beyond the

few short years intervening between our national elections, is, to say the least, a pitiable spectacle. To
excite this state of apprehension and uncertainty is a
part of the demagogues' plan of campaign; to work
up a crisis and produce if possible a political panic
has a wonderful effect in producing changes in the
popular vote. Politicians are most active and hopeful
in a period of business depression and calamity.
When crops are short, when prices rise or fall, when
there is discontent and violence among laborers, when
values shrink enormously and bankruptcies are plenty,
such a state of things is in the nature of a Godsend
to a faction in the minority. Parties thrive on the
misfortunes of the country, and they work the calamity rôle for all it is worth to drive the ignorant and
timid into the political fold.

These professional agitators of political issues are
to the voting population at large just what the walk-
ing delegates and the master workman, who works
only with his mandibles, are to the laboring class:
marauding wool-gatherers, who cry wolf to frighten
and stampede the human flock that they may the
more successfully tithe and tax them, solely for the
profit of the placemen who rule them. They are the
greatest enemies to the diversified industries and the
business interests of the nation that it has had to
contend with in modern times. They have absorbed
the public attention and disturbed the public peace
for generations in these stale discussions and boot-
less campaigns of affirmation and denial, and taxed
the strength and resources of the nation in main-

taining a hostile feeling and inciting a factional
quarrel between citizens and neighbors in every
hamlet in the land. To what good end have they
succeeded in confusing the public mind and debauching the public conscience? In this endless debate all the questions involved are to the people the
profoundest mysteries. The question of the currency
is as mysterious to the average voter as the ways of
Providence; and the tariff is a labyrinth in which
partisan statesmanship has been groping for generations without finding its clue.

CHAPTER XXI.

HOW THEY SPEND THEIR OWN MONEY AND OTHER PEOPLE'S TIME.

WE may obtain some idea of the magnitude of
these associations and the interest felt in their general success by those who support them, if we note
the amount of money they contribute in aid of them.
A political party is a very expensive institution, and
when it is mobilized for a Presidential campaign it
requires plenty of money, which must be liberally
disbursed. The amount of money they annually
misapply and waste, so far as any benefit is derived
from it to the country at large, is enormous. If
they were patriotic and useful organizations, as they
claim to be, spending time and money unselfishly for

the public good, if they were not preying upon the resources of the country, obstructing its material progress and distracting its civil and industrial policy, the public would have little concern in the matter of their expenditures for party support; but as organized conspiracies against the general welfare, who tax the people to supply the means for their own vassalage and degradation, it is well to know what they are doing by the use of money to maintain the authority they have usurped over the nation.

The spending of large sums of money by any association organized for selfish purposes and against public policy furnishes evidence at least that the enterprise is a profitable one, and that the contributors expect in some way to be reimbursed for their timely advances. The bulk of the money spent by the great parties is for the purpose of successfully carrying the elections of the country. As the most of this money is spent in a secret or more or less private way, over a wide extent of the national domain, we have no means of knowing, proximately even, what is thus widely scattered throughout the election districts of the country. We have some reliable knowledge, however, of the large amounts disbursed for conducting Presidential campaigns and holding nominating conventions. These show the clearest indications of their masterful possession of the political field, and the resources they can command to maintain their supremacy as the power paramount in the land.

The Republican Convention of 1896, held at St. Louis, which nominated Mr. McKinley for President, is said to have cost the party and its friends four million dollars. I gather this estimate from Republican sources, and I think it is perhaps reliable. This sum included the hall in which the convention assembled, which was erected for that special purpose and cost not far from seventy-five thousand dollars. This sum also included the large disbursements of one sergeant-at-arms for various purposes and the expenses of a hundred thousand visitors to the city on the occasion. The railroad fare of the delegates is estimated at eight hundred thousand dollars, and the fare of the visitors at a much larger sum, while the estimate for their maintenance is put at over two million dollars. These sums, together with the amounts paid for telegraphing, music, servant hire, maintaining State headquarters, etc., make up an aggregate of about four millions which it cost the party to nominate their Presidential candidate. The value of the time lost by all these attendants upon the gathering does not appear in this estimate. The conducting of the political campaign in which Mr. McKinley and Mr. Bryan were rivals it is said cost the two parties, in disbursements made under the direction of the two National Committees severally, another four million dollars. The New York *World* of November 16, 1896, had this to say about the cost of the campaign:

"The Presidential campaign just closed cost the Republican and Democratic National Committees alone more than two million five hundred thousand dollars. Chairman Hanna had at his command over one million four hundred thousand dollars. The Democratic National Committee fund was nearly as large. The five silver-producing States and the mine-owners raised three-fourths of all the money Chairman Jones spent. For the first time in twenty years the Republican National Committee completed its work, paid all its debts, and had a surplus. Money flowed into the Republican coffers from the East. The West gave little or nothing except to its State organizations. Chicago bankers devoted most of their spare funds to their State machine, which had troubles of its own in its fight with Altgeld. The moneyed men of St. Louis were a source of grave disappointment to the National Committee, owing to their small contributions. From the East the big contributions in round numbers were as follows:

New York	$500,000
Philadelphia	475,000
Pittsburg	250,000
Boston	162,000
Scattering	75,000
Total	$1,462,000

"No national committee ever had such enormous financial resources at its disposal, and never before has there been so much money spent in legitimate campaigning in the way of speakers, campaign literature, etc. The dissemination of literature was the heaviest item of expense. This was practically all done through the Chicago bureau, presided over by Perry Heath. Through this bureau there were sent out in one of the biggest weeks of the campaign

thirty million documents by mail, each piece covered
with a two cent stamp. This meant an expenditure
of six hundred thousand dollars for postage alone.
These are large figures, but they are not worrying
some Republicans nearly as much as the question of
what will become of the balance on hand in the National Committee coffers. If reports are true, there
was a national committee which solved a similar
problem not a great many years ago by dividing up
some forty thousand dollars among the head-quarters
leaders the day before the election, and that was
why the committee had to carry a small debt for
four years more.] What the Republican and Democratic State and local committees spent during the
campaign it is next to impossible to ascertain, but
it is estimated that it would amount to fully half as
much as that expended in the conduct of the national
campaign. The aggregate of the election expenses
was close to four million dollars, more than enough
to keep up the English royal establishment. The
civic list of Queen Victoria, together with the an-
nuities paid to the royal family, amount yearly to
only $2,742,845."

Now, if we add to this record the large sums spent
in sustaining local organizations and endeavors to
carry local elections throughout the country, we have
a very large aggregate of money spent and time
wasted in sustaining these endless controversies between rival political factions. What practical good
does the nation derive from this display of energy
and cunning in the political sphere? [For many
months previous to a Presidential election the country is filled with excitement, and resounds from the
Atlantic to the Pacific with the voice of the cam-

paigner; business is partially suspended and waits the decision of the great national prize-fight between the two leading parties. They call it a campaign of education. It is not, for the people learn nothing new nor settle anything practically by these pro and con discussions. They are merely campaigns of controversy and polemics, a war of words and the reiteration of the stale platitudes and feeble pleasantries of the average demagogue.⟩

Suppose those respectable Christian sects, the Presbyterians and the Baptists of this country, should inaugurate a national campaign of education to discuss before the people for a period of several months the distinctive differences in their several creeds. No doubt the people would hear reiterated many valuable Bible truths, but who would be enlightened or made better by such a sectarian controversy? Would any progress be made in settling the merits of this debate which has existed for centuries between the sects? By the experience and good sense of all Christendom such public wrangling has long since been condemned.

The parties use these public gatherings more as a means of exciting enthusiasm in their own ranks, and keeping their voting force well in hand for election day, than from any expectation that they are to change the views of the public on current party issues by speeches and campaign literature. They have so confused the public mind by their "damnable iterations," that the people have little interest really in their elocution or their literature. They

are overwhelmed with words and phrases, with affir-
mations and denials, until they hardly know what
to believe or who to trust. Time was when figures
did not lie, and statistics were of some value in ascer-
taining the true condition of the country and the
state of trade, and deducing from them a settled
policy for the business of the country. Now, the
politician of each side will take the same data and
undertake to demonstrate the certainty of opposite
conclusions. Prevarication and perversion have become distinctively political methods, so that from the
same state of facts each party will show that it embodies well-nigh all the wisdom, patriotism and
humanity in the country, that to them is due all the
prosperity the nation has ever enjoyed or ever will
enjoy. As a result of these tactics, a large class of
citizens are so confused and perplexed, so beset by
candidates and bosses, that in a sort of desperation
they follow the last sensation, the biggest crowd, and
the loudest drum beat, and are sincerely gratified
and greatly relieved when the excitement and bulldozing of the campaign is over.

The waste of time as well as the waste of money
is a noteworthy item in the people's account against
these alliances. This is very large from the red-tape
methods that everywhere prevail in the public service, and in no direction is it more conspicuous than
in the national Congress, where the delay of public
business and needed legislation add largely to the
inconvenience and damage the country suffers from
the present partisan rule of public affairs.

The difference between the time necessary to carry on a government non-partisan and harmonious in character and that of an administration of it when involved in all the antagonisms and diversions incident to party strife is very great. Political parties are the most wasteful and indolent of servants. If time is money, then they have wasted millions by diverting the time and service they owe the government to their own use and profit. The delay of public business in Congress is a subject of universal complaint. That some four hundred men shall remain in session for seven or eight months with ten thousand bills before them requiring attention, and accomplish little or nothing satisfactory to the public, is evidence either of their incompetency or the wilful neglect of their duties as representatives of the people. The greater part of the time of this body seems to be occupied in endeavors to make political capital out of pending legislation and in mutual detraction and disparagement. No man can make a speech in either house that it does not assume a partisan character, and the chances are it will bring on a lengthy discussion of party measures. Days, and sometimes weeks are spent in these wranglings. It would seem that a member of that body cannot open his mouth without in some way attempting to glorify or defend his party or assail his political opponent. It is notoriously true, and a matter well understood by all concerned, that each short session is to be devoted to politics and party skirmishing rather than to the business of legislation.

Here is an extract from the correspondence of the

Associated Press, written in anticipation of the assembling of the short session of the Fifty-third Congress. It reads:

"The approaching session of Congress, which will convene on December 5, is not expected by those familiar with Congressional methods to be one of great activity or productive of much legislation. The fact that it continues for only three months, that it will be the last session of the Congress, and that it so closely follows a general election, are all considered as indications that comparatively little work will be attempted and still less accomplished. The greater part of the session will, in all probability, be confined to an exchange of chaffing over the results of the election, and the session will be commemorable more on account of talk than work. It is probable that next to nothing will be done from the Christmas holidays, and predictions are freely made that it will be difficult to obtain a quorum previous to Christmas. After the holidays there will be but two months left for work and speech-making. It will be, of course, necessary to pass the usual appropriations. These bills touch a variety of interests, and while on this occasion they will be disposed of with considerable alacrity, they can always be so manipulated as to kill much time when there is any considerable element which desires to rouse them."

By report of the Secretary of the Treasury for the fiscal year 1895 the annual expenses of the two houses of Congress is $7,639,166.65, or something over twenty thousand dollars a day. Add to this the loss and inconvenience to the business of the country by such profligacy on the part of its representatives, and we find a partisan Congress is a very expensive institution.

This is our indictment of the great popular alliances of the day known as political parties, these monster conspiracies against the autonomy of the Republic. We ask the reader in all sincerity if it is not true in every count? We may have extenuated in charity, but we have set down naught in malice or in party prejudice. We have endeavored, first, to be truthful, next, impartial, and always to be just in dealing with facts and forces which we could but condemn. We believe that what we have written in censure of the politicians of the country, their organizations and their methods generally, is in accordance with the public judgment, and is sustained by almost a popular clamor for relief from their tyranny. We think we have conclusively shown that the public derives no substantial benefit from these clannish associations, that they are of no practical value to the nation, and that really we have no possible use for their services. On the contrary, it is sucessfully maintained that they are, from their general character and the selfish motives which influence and control their action, wholly incapacitated for any other mission than that of a disturbing force in the body politic, wasting its revenues and degrading the public service. A few hundred thousand men are benefited by this system of spoliation and organized presumption. The office-holders, government contractors, and those who obtain legislation by unlawful means are its chief beneficiaries and its most earnest and liberal supporters. There

is not one man in a hundred of the voters of all the
parties who obtains any of these special benefits, or
has any real interest in the maintenance of these organizations. Seventy millions of people are suffering
immense losses annually in every branch of industry
and every material interest, and are taxed, harassed,
and despoiled for the benefit of the few who have
usurped all authority, hold the reins of government,
and are the predominant power in the nation.

CHAPTER XXII.

THE REMEDY.

It would seem that an evil of such magnitude
should have a remedy. To say that there is none
within the sphere of prohibitory laws is to acknowl-
edge a fatal defect in the scheme of representative
government. It is a public wrong and one that
threatens the integrity of our political system, if not
its complete failure and disruption. The very nature
of the evil is suggestive of a remedy by appropriate
legislation. All its concomitants are recognized as
more or less the subjects of legislative action and control. The party methods form the general ground of
complaint of the people against these political unions.
They involve acts of fraud, violence, and corruption,
which are a violation of law and are so declared by
statute in every State in the Union when committed by

individuals. Any citizen who stuffs a ballot-box, repeats his vote, purchases the vote of another, or who is guilty of bribery or intimidation of voters is liable to indictment and prosecution by the State. Now, when these individual acts become the recognized methods of an association, of a grand conspiracy to seize and use the entire powers of the commonwealth for its own benefit, are they any less violations of law, or are they any the less deserving of merited punishment? Why should they not alike be amenable to law? Should such associations, which are the chief agencies through which these crimes are successfully committed, who give asylum and rewards to the guilty, continue to be regarded as beyond the reach of law and such restraining and wholesome legislation as the interests of the public may require?

The right to vote and hold any office of honor and emolument, the freedom of the ballot, and the purity of elections by the people are fundamental rights of citizenship, and as such are regulated and abundantly guarded by law. The people are entitled to the protection of their rights by the enforcement of these laws against all alliances and conspiracies as well as against individuals. All infringements upon the free exercise of these sacred privileges of citizenship and all combinations to defeat or hinder such lawful use of them are in every free country the subjects of legislation; and a government who fails to protect its people in the exercise of these high prerogatives of citizenship is not wisely administered. It is true, if all the voters of a State would cease to co-operate with and support the present political organizations, there would be an end of them very speedily in such locality, but so long as a small minority is permitted to combine to gain political power, there will be need, in aid of the majority, of some provision of law that will exclude such confederations and their agents from all the competitive contests of the political field.

As I have already shown, conclusively I think, elsewhere, so long as political power and the spoils of office are to be gained as at present through the machinery of party organization, such combinations will exist and find abundant support. They will never disband from the force of public sentiment or die of their inherent corruptions. A law declaring any candidate nominated by any such political association ineligible to the office for which he is designated would restore the elective power to the hands of the people individually and protect them from the corrupting influence and competition of the present powerful parties. The offices are intended for competent and responsible citizens who are chosen by individual ballots to represent and serve the people, and not for the bosses and master workmen of the political machine. No combination or device should be tolerated which will defeat or corrupt a fair distribution of the honors and emoluments of places of trust in the public service. This remedy would rule the parties as such out of the political field. The offices are the prizes to be won, they are the source of spoils and the key to the situation. Prohibited from competing with the people for these responsible positions they would be left without occupation or a sufficient inducement to maintain such an organization under such restrictions. They would have neither race-course nor tilting-ground on which they could contest with one another for the honors of office and the right to govern and plunder the people as of yore.

The remedy here suggested is simple in form, covers the malady, and I think would prove more effective than a more elaborate and prohibitive provision of law, needlessly antagonizing these organizations. When the majority of the voting population of any sovereign State decides to free the commonwealth from the incubus of party domination let the Legislature declare by statute in some such form as this:

The freedom of election, the purity of the ballot, and the unrestrained voice of the citizen in the election of those who shall represent him are primal rights of citizenship, and must be neither hindered nor impaired. That all political associations or parties organized or maintained for the purpose of nominating or electing candidates for public office, or of influencing or controlling elections in the State, or seeking to control and distribute the public patronage for the use and benefit of such associations are hostile in their influence and tendency to our free institutions, and should be disfellowshipped and condemned by all good citizens. That long experience in this country with those combinations known as political parties has shown that the tendency of their influence and operations is to trans-

12

fer permanently the sovereignty of the individual
citizen to an irresponsible and often a corrupt and
dangerous faction, who will use it unscrupulously
for their own political advancement. Such action
on the part of any combination of citizens for such
purpose is hereby declared unlawful and dangerous
to the liberties of the people. And it is further provided, more effectually to restrain the improper action of these parties and free the commonwealth
from their baneful influence, that any person chosen
or nominated to office by such organizations shall not
be eligible to the offices to which they are thus
nominated or chosen. That nothing herein con-
tained shall be so construed as to prohibit or restrain
the people of the State from assembling together
and freely discussing questions of public policy and
expressing their opinions and preferences as to candidates for public office.

The moral force of such an attitude on the part
of the constituted authorities and a majority of the
citizens of a State would be in a high degree effica-
cious if not altogether remedial in its influence.
That, together with the interdiction of barring the
parties from the privilege heretofore enjoyed of
filling the offices with their own agents and partisans
to the exclusion of all others, could but prove effective in ridding the public speedily of their presence.
Under such restrictions how would they get their
candidates before the people? Candidates must be
duly proclaimed and endorsed to obtain the party
vote. Who would know, but a few, who was the

accepted aspirant for office of the combination? Interested parties would be ready to create doubt and confusion as to the fact, and the burden of secrecy imposed upon such a movement would not only be impracticable, but one too great to be borne.

There is no necessity to attempt through any provision of law directly to suppress these conclaves, or to restrain them in the exercise of those rights which are generally conceded to all voluntary associations which do not by their teachings or their practices deprave the public morals or endanger the public safety. Such prohibitive measures might raise a variety of questions connected with the execution of the law which would serve only as pretext for hindering or delaying the enforcement of the act. If the remedy here suggested should prove either in theory or practice inadequate or incompetent, there could be no reasonable doubt as to the power of a Legislature to protect the administration of government and the rights of the people against all such combinations and conspiracies to waste their revenues and rob them of their autonomy. I do not foresee any serious obstacles to the successful administration of such a law. Some questions of the interpretation of the statutes might arise, but I apprehend that they would be soon settled by investigation of the facts involved, or by the court if the necessity required such *dernier ressort.*

Let us suppose some such case as this, and perhaps others collateral to it might arise: A. B. claims to have been elected as a member of the State Legislature and demands a certificate of his election. Previous to the election some days or weeks a large public meeting of voters was held in the county where he resides, and at which he was present and took a conspicuous part. He was known at the time to be a candidate for the office and had so announced himself in the newspapers of the county. At that meeting there were present and active members of the old parties, as well as citizens who were zealous non-partisans. Public measures and the merits of various candidates were freely discussed. A. B. was called upon to state his views in regard to certain local questions of interest to those present. When the meeting adjourned, as it did, *sine die*, it seemed pretty well understood and settled that A. B. was the choice of the meeting for member of Assembly, and that he would be elected on voting day. This general expectation was fully realized, as he had a large majority of the votes in the district in his favor.

Now, those who were opposed to A. B.'s election alleged against him the following state of facts: They declared that he was a Republican, a member of the party and always had been, though of a moderate type; that he was put forward in the canvas by the local party for the office as their choice, and had been elected mainly by Republican votes; that the meeting named was called and organized by the local members of the party for the purpose of presenting A. B. before the people of the district and obtaining such action on their part as would be in effect a nomination by the meeting. Though no formal nomination had been presented, the Republican party had accomplished through the meeting all the purposes and benefits of an ordinary nomination by the body, and hence A. B.'s accession to the office would be a fraud upon the non-partisan act made and provided in such cases. This contention, if persisted in, might be carried into the courts as a last resort. It would there, and elsewhere, be a simple matter of evidence whether these allegations were sustained, and whether within the meaning and intent of the statute he was nominated as the candidate of a political combination or party.

Such cases of contested elections are very common, and the courts are constantly adjudicating questions arising out of them. The legislation here proposed would not involve anything difficult in legal interpretation, or new in judicial decisions. There would no doubt be many attempts to evade the law, and some of them would be successful for a time, but no party could long stand the strain of the necessary vigilance and labor to keep up a warfare of such magnitude and imminent risk as would be involved in a twofold contest with rival organizations on the one hand, and with the friends and forces of the law on the other. The load of public odium and distrust which they already carry would seemingly be increased beyond endurance even by politicians.

CHAPTER XXIII.

OBJECTIONS.

OBJECTIONS to the views I have taken of this question may naturally arise in the minds of many persons to whom the subject has been presented. Some of these I shall venture to anticipate, and make such reply to them as I think should be satisfactory to the unprejudiced reader of these pages. A standing objection, and generally a leading one, to every measure of reform is that it is impracticable and really impossible. It will be said in this case that there can be little hope of such a reform as is here urged, because the people will not sustain it; that they are pledged and bound almost unanimously to the rule of the parties who are so firmly intrenched in public favor and by actual possession that they cannot be routed.

Many men will content themselves with such an objection to what is here advanced, and perhaps with a pish of contempt dismiss from their minds the whole subject. I confess that I cannot answer this objection in any satisfactory form. The answer lies with each citizen who has a vote to cast. If you and I resolve that we will no longer act with or sustain any political organization in the nature of the present parties, that meets the objection for each of us; and if a majority of the voters will do the same the reform will be accomplished. It is not worth while to waste words in

reply to the man who meets every measure of progress
or reform with the disparaging cry, "It won't succeed;
it can't be done." I have no assistance to offer such
a citizen in his helplessness and despair. He is a political Ephraim; he is joined to his idols, and we will
let him alone; better men will do his work for him and
his children. There is no slavery more abject than
that of a man who has no aspirations for freedom,
and has lost all hope for himself and his country.
They are everywhere the drones of the social hive and
the enemies of human progress.

Another objection more plausible and yet more
easily disposed of may very likely be urged. It may
be said that the legislation here proposed will be a
violation of the rights of the people to assemble and
take such concerted action as they may deem advisable
in regard to public measures, to select candidates for
office of their choice and holding their own opinions,
and recommending them to the confidence and support of their fellow-citizens generally. Section 10
of the Constitution of California provides that the
people shall have the right to freely assemble together
to consult for the common good, to instruct their representatives, and to petition the Législature for redress
of grievances. It will be alleged that to refuse a citizen the right to be presented to the public and be thus
recommended and nominated by his friends is to virtually deny him the right to hold office, and, in fact,
to disfranchise an innocent person, for the right to
hold office is a collateral right with that of casting a
vote.

In reply to this we say, first, the legislation here contemplated does not seek to restrain the people in their rights to assemble in large or small bodies for po· litical purposes to hold such discussions as they may see fit, and even formally to nominate for office such persons as they may choose, and urge others to vote for such candidates of their own choice and opinions. The proposed remedy simply provides that when such candidates are formally nominated as the representatives of some political association, they shall not be eligible to the office for which they may be elected. Political gatherings may be held, and nominating conventions may exercise their functions to any extent, but it does not follow that all such candidates are deprived of their rights because they are not permitted under the circumstances to hold office. Neither have the persons who have formally put them before the people and urged their election been unduly restrained of their freedom as citizens. The governments of all nations reserve to themselves the right to determine the qualifications and general character of those who hold office under their patronage, as well as the circumstances attendant, and the methods employed in securing their accession to office. It is found necessary that each department of the government, executive, legislative, and judicial, should be largely vested with this power for its own protection.

Secondly, we say that the right to vote and to hold office are not absolute but conditional rights. Everybody cannot vote; everybody cannot hold office. There are reasons why many worthy citizens may not enjoy these privileges. Even citizens who have not committed crime may be under such disabilities and prohibitions that they can neither vote nor hold office. No man who was born in a foreign country can be President of the United States. A man may be a citizen and a voter and not eligible for the office of Representative in Congress because he is under twenty-five years of age; or has not resided for fourteen years in the country and is thirty-five years of age. A person engaged in trade and commerce is not eligible to the office of Secretary of the United States Treasury. The citizens of the District of Columbia have not the elective franchise, though they may hold office. The women of the country, though citizens, are not permitted to vote in a large majority of the States of the Union. In some of the States there is a property qualification, and in others a requirement that the voter must be able to read and write. These are not natural but conventional rights. You have no natural right to vote or hold office in every community where you see fit to remove. A citizen removing from California to New York will remain without the right to vote to the end of his days unless he takes the steps required by the laws of New York to make him a voter in that State.

Thus, not always on grounds of principle, but often of policy and expediency, men are denied these privileges. So the Legislature, in the discharge of its duty to provide for the general welfare and protect the State from any invasion or usurpation of its authority, may disfranchise a citizen even and deny him the high privilege of holding an office of honor and trust under the government, notably those who have been convicted of treason and rebellion, or who have conspired to seize or overthrow the constituted authorities. Revolutionists, anarchists, and socialists, all over the civilized world, are subjects of discriminating legislation, as persons who menace established order of society and seek to usurp by force or fraud, if need be, the powers of the government and the rule of the people.

There has been much power exercised in the history of free governments in the disfranchisement of voting citizens and debarring them from holding office, most of which may not be satisfactorily defended; nevertheless, all governments must protect their people in the exercise of their rights and from the conspiracies of bad men to absorb for themselves the powers and emoluments of the commonwealth. Suppose a large majority of the people of a State should inaugurate a grand lottery scheme, by which the elections to office would be made to yield a large revenue to the State treasury. Suppose that this device provided that all offices from governor down should be listed as prizes and drawn for after the fashion of an old-time Louisiana lottery, those drawing prizes having pledges and assurance of an election on voting day. Suppose the result of the scheme showed that a great many people lost money in this sort of office-hunting, and that the prime movers and managers of the project drew all the prizes. Would not the Legislature have power to deal with such a practice and break up such a combination, or declare such nominees ineligible, or that all persons engaged in pool-selling, book-making, and betting on elections were not eligible to office? This plan comprises many features of the present method of selecting candidates for office and procuring their election, and would hardly be less dangerous and demoralizing to the public service. Each State has the power to prohibit lotteries and gambling generally. Why not gambling and lotteries in the sphere of politics where such practices are far more reprehensible and pernicious in their influence? No intelligent people will long permit any combination to usurp civil or military powers of the State and use them for their own advantage under any pretence whatever. A wise and efficient government would not delay action when its authority was menaced until revolutionists should strike their first blow, or a grand conspiracy had by easy stages corrupted the civil service and been thus enabled to seize and defiantly hold the plenary powers of the nation.

Section 26 of Article IV. of the Constitution of California provides as follows: "The Legislature shall pass laws to prohibit the sale in this State of lottery or gift enterprise tickets, or tickets in any scheme in the nature of a lottery. The Legislature shall pass laws to regulate or prohibit the buying and selling of the shares of capital stock of corporations in any stock board, stock exchange, or stock market under the control of any association. All contracts for the sale of shares of the capital stock of any corporation or association, on margin or to be delivered at a future day, shall be void."

The power of the Legislature to deal with all associations, political, social, or religious, which endanger the public peace or usurp authority, civil or military, over any community, is generally conceded. The pretensions set forth and the demand made upon society by the various confraternities of agitators who threaten the existing order of things the world over have called the attention of the public to the question of their restraint or suppression by the force of law. These opinions have been variously expressed, and some of them in European states have taken the form of statutes to be enforced against those who degrade the morals of society or menace the public safety.

I find in the New York daily *Tribune* of November 16, 1894, an interview of Ex-Senator Warner Miller, of New York, on the result of the fall elections. His language abundantly sustains the view I have taken of the power of the Legislature over these corrupt and dangerous political associations. The Senator was asked, "What in your judgment ought to be done with Tammany Hall?" He replied as follows:

"I said, two years ago, repeal its charter. I repeat that now. I know that its charter covers a so-called charitable society, but the name has become a synonyme for corruption of every form in municipal government. Therefore, legislate the name out of existence. But don't stop at that. Pass a law which will prevent the printing of tickets of any secret or semi-secret organization which is self-perpetuating.

Allow tickets to be printed only for open, free, political organizations of the party, such as town, county, and State conventions give; and any ticket made in whole or in part by secret organizations should be prevented by law from being voted at the polls. It was secret societies and cabals which so long threatened republican government in France. They have always been dangerous to free institutions. Therefore, make it impossible that any secret or semi-secret organization shall become a controlling power in this country. I am very sure that the lawyers of this city will be able to frame a bill to carry out this suggestion."

I think these remarks are quite applicable to Senator Platt's Tammany faction of the Republican party in that State, quite as applicable to the notorious cabal of political freebooters he has organized, with whom he seems to be making common cause in sustaining the spoils system and opposing all genuine reform in the Empire State. This sort of thing is evidently hastening a political crisis in the great Commonwealth, the legitimate outcome of which must be the destruction of civil liberty or the annihilation of these powerful confederations of ambition and intrigue.

It will be said, furthermore, in opposition to this mode of reform, that these parties are organizations of the people, and contain well-nigh all the voters of the country; that the people choose to act politically through such organizations; that it is a chosen and long-established method of expressing themselves in regard to public men and measures; that they are so identified with these forms of political action that

it may be said that the people are the party and the
party are the people. They very confidently inquire
who has a right to complain of it? There is truth in
this objection; and the people have a right to act
through any organization they may choose, and adopt
any forms or methods in administering the government for which they are responsible that seem to them
wisest and best. They may choose any form of government, or decide to be anarchists and have no government at all if that suits the popular idea of social
order. We fully recognize the sovereign right of the
people to be represented by a party or any other political agency they may select; but when such choice is
hindered and defeated at the polls or elsewhere, by
the fraudulent devices of the agent or representative
body, and that body becomes self-perpetuating and
abuses the authority it has usurped, it should be repudiated and displaced forever as untrustworthy.
Such a form of representation has such inherent defects and such corrupting tendencies as to make it a
dangerous and inadmissible agency in civil administration. They undoubtedly have the right to choose
such a medium of representation, but so much the
worse for the people if they make such an unfortunate
choice in the exercise of it.

This unwise use of their sovereignty by a majority
of the voters cannot deprive the minority of their
rights to protest and to labor for a better administration of public affairs. Nor is it a sufficient answer
to their allegation of facts, showing the depraved
condition of our political system and the necessity

of its radical improvement. That the great majority of the people of this country are supporting this monstrous conspiracy against good government, and that they will oppose stubbornly any genuine reform in this direction, is nothing new in the history of civilized society. All the great wrongs that have overshadowed and blighted the happiness of our race have been permitted and fostered by the great mass of the people. The wisdom of experience is not always the best wisdom, nor is the voice of the people always the voice of God.

In discussing this subject with various persons I have found those who raise an objection to discarding altogether the old parties, on the ground that they embody pretty much all the talent and experience available in the country for political purposes; that they, besides, have an organized system of administering government and facilitating its labors that can hardly be dispensed with unless we can have assurance of something better in its place. They ask, How will you reach the ears of the people to instruct them on important questions upon which they are called to act, if there are no parties to inaugurate campaigns of discussion and education? How can you select proper candidates for office or hold elections without the aid of party zeal, party money, and party machinery? They really believe that these organizations are indispensable to the successful administration of the government of the United States, as well as government of the several States of the Union. There are a great many peo-

ple in the world who hold much the same views
in regard to kingcraft and human slavery. It seems
to them impossible that the world could be successfully governed without kings to rule the people, and
they hope for nothing but anarchy and bloodshed
when slaves are enfranchised.

The political parties have in some respects been
useful to the country; if they had not been they
would not have been tolerated down to the present
day, with all their frailties and transgressions of the
moral law. They have had their uses as all great
evils have. An unmitigated public wrong, one that
does not confer substantial benefits upon any class
of society, will be without patrons to defend it, and
will soon be suppressed at the hands of those who
most suffer from it. It is too late in the history
of civilization to insist upon the doctrine that there
can be no church without a bishop, no state without
a king, or that there can be no commonwealth without the aid of political parties. We contend that the
present parties exert no salutary or wholesome influence upon public opinion, which they seek so
earnestly and diligently to control. They have no
sphere of usefulness in any community, great or
small. Neither society nor civil government has
any proper use for them, and they should wholly
dispense with their pretensions and their services, so
persistently thrust upon them, at the earliest day
possible. They burden rather than facilitate the
legitimate labors of the commonwealth. The system
of administration that they have established in this

country is not only defective in a multitude of ways, but has become so complicated and cumbrous that at times and places its functions seem well-nigh suspended. It is cumbrous and complex much for the reason that the gates and doors of prisons are made of iron, with locks and combinations that are a puzzle to the average mind. The people inside have the reputation of being rascals, and they need a stronger government and more of it than honest people do. When a government has been practically let on shares for many years, as a farmer lets his acres, the suspicions and vigilance of the parties will lead them to build up a system of administration, offensive and defensive, and more or less complicated and amplified. There will needs be much red tape and many checks and balances introduced to maintain the equilibrium of the contending forces. There must be a vast detective system, a "circumlocution office," and numerous experts in the science of "how not to do it."

Many persons suppose that our appliances for holding elections, giving a publicity to the time and place of holding them, designating competent men to fill the offices, furnishing polling places and ballots at their own expense, haranguing the people and securing the attendance of the largest number of them at the polls,—that all these devices are the invention of the parties, a system which their genius has supplied and their patriotism supports; and without their assistance in putting this machinery in operation the government would have to provide other agents and agencies in carrying on this important work, and even then suffer serious embarrassment from the change.

This is an entire misapprehension of the subject. While the parties are not wholly ignored in our theory and form of government, State and national, they are not recognized except, incidentally, as agencies necessary or otherwise in carrying on the government of the several States or of the nation at large. They perform no service for the government or the people that would not at once be improved if they would cease their persistence in volunteering it and withdraw from it altogether. That they afford the public any aid in the management of elections and the choice of candidates is notoriously untrue. There are constitutional provisions or express statutes in all the States that provide all the necessary machinery for popular elections with a full vote and a fair count, so that the people do not need the assistance of the politicians and the partisans who harass and harangue them through their interminable campaigns. The election laws, for example, of our own State of California are full and specific in their provisions, so that no citizen need be dependent on any other aid or instruction in the discharging of his duties as a voter than that which is furnished in the most intelligent and practical manner by the statutes and the official persons of the State. Thirty days before a general election the governor issues a proclamation announcing the event. Copies of this document are sent to the supervisors of the counties where such elections are to be held, stating the day of such election and the offices to be filled. The supervisors have this printed in the newspapers of the county and posted at each place where an election is to be held. The necessary printed blanks for poll lists, lists of voters, oaths, and returns are furnished by the Board of Supervisors to the officers of each election precinct at the expense of the county. The law defines who shall be voters, and provides for their registration previous to the election, posting up copies of the same and supplying them to all persons who apply for them. The Board of Supervisors having charge and control of elections divide the counties and cities into precincts containing not more than two hundred voters. The supervisors designate the place in the precinct where the election must be held and the officers to be elected. They also appoint two inspectors, two judges, and two clerks; these six constitute a Board of Election for such precinct. The time of opening and closing the polls is prescribed by the law, and such opening and closing are proclaimed aloud at the time. The law defines what is a ticket and what is a ballot, or secret ticket, and that it must be of paper, uniform in size, color, weight, texture, and appearance. The Secretary of State provides this paper and prescribes the size of the ticket, the kind of type and ink to be used, and gives a form or model of the ticket to be voted and the manner of folding it. Very full instruction is given as to the specific manner of voting and to receiving and depositing the votes. There are also a large number of provisions in the law touching and regulating the challenge of votes and the trials of the same. Then follow a great number of clauses as to the counting of votes and declaring the result. This return must be sent to the Secretary of State, whose duty it is to compare and estimate the votes given, and certify to the governor the person having the highest number of votes. The governor on receipt of this report sends to each person chosen a certificate of the election.

These are substantially the election laws of all the States of the Union. I have given this detailed account of them to correct the impression among a class of voters who never seek to inform themselves as to their political duties, who suppose that our elective system is so complicated that nobody but the politicians have mastered it, and that they are about the only safe interpreters of its provisions. There are thousands of honest voters acting under such false impressions who have become quite helpless, and have surrendered themselves implicitly to the canvassers and whippers-in of their party. The interference of these organizations with the responsibilities of the voting citizens is altogether gratuitous and impudent, it being, as a general thing, neither solicited nor needed by those who are subjected to it. One might as well submit his business affairs to the intrusion and superintendence of an association, with the right to harass and tax him through the year on pretence of protecting and improving his business.

Let us suppose that a general election is about to be held in a State; that a governor, a lieutenant-governor, and members of the Senate and the Assembly are to be chosen, together with some officers of the judiciary. Let us further suppose that there are no political parties in existence in the State. Now, what would be the natural course of political events in connection with this election? Any intelligent citizen could predict them with a good degree of certainty, from his knowledge of the fact that there is a love of order, justice, and fair play in the strife of politics even among the people that will change the character of our popular elections as soon as they are relieved of the presence of party methods and party dictation. He would not apprehend loss or damage to the State or the community from the fact that it was not a party election, an old time competitive contest between several giant organizations for place and power. What would the voting population do under these circumstances? What else would there be to do but to vote and retire to their homes? If there were questions of local interest involved in the canvass, like woman's suffrage, the manufacture and sale of intoxicants, or, in case of a Presidential election, national questions, like the tariff, or the currency, should be exciting much discussion and interest among the people, the friends of the measures who were sufficiently in earnest about them to hold public discussions and circulate views would naturally do so, though they were not partisans. All those better methods now in use of

instructing and arousing the people and calling out
a decisive vote on election day would be continued
by those in favor of progress and reform in civil
affairs. These reformers might if they chose, emu-
late the zeal and liberality of the old parties in inaugurating campaigns of rhetoric and elocution,
adorned with music and banners, so at one and the
same time both please and capture the voting public.

Under these new conditions there would be no necessity of hunting up that class of men who never
asked for office and whose nominations were a surprise to them, and urging them to accommodate the
public and their friends by accepting a lucrative
place for a term of years. There would be no lack
of candidates, and of a class quite different from the
present style of office-seekers. The press would deal
with all these matters of political interest with
scarcely less zeal than they descant upon party questions at the present time. The newspapers, relieved
from party surveillance and dictation, would be a
far more reliable source of information on political
topics than they are now. The people generally
would be better informed on these subjects than
heretofore, and their discussions and reading, freed
from party bias, would be more deliberate and sincere. The public judgment as expressed at the polls
would be the verdict of the people, and not the
triumph of one cabal over another. Its decisions
would be based upon justice and the common weal,
and not on party fealty and party dictation. It would
not be a party election where men *en masse* vote for

measures prescribed by a party platform and little comprehended by the average voter, giving a tacit but not a cordial assent, surrendering their judgments for the purpose of party harmony and success. Every citizen would be at liberty to study these questions without bias or dictation and vote for such persons and measures as he may choose, thus securing to every man a fair opportunity to vote his convictions without fraud or intimidation.

With the partisan element discarded and ruled out of our political system, the whole character of the political drama, varying as it now does from farce to tragedy, would be changed. Instead of strife, distrust, and corruption on every hand, the political field would become a scene of peaceful co-operation and emulative zeal among the people, to make and preserve for themselves and their children the best government under the sun. Such a change as is here suggested would bring an entire new class of men into the sphere of political activity; patriotic and public-spirited citizens, who are now overslawed and shouldered out of public life by venal politicians and placemen, would find room for their honest endeavors in the way of reform. This better class of citizens, found in every walk of life, have essayed bravely from time to time to stay the tide of demoralization and corruption flowing from this source, but everywhere they find the people captured and enslaved by the party organization, and they have generally retired from all political activity in disgust, convinced that any reform of our current

political methods is a labor without hope. With the
rights of the people restored, and the elective franchise relieved from the surveillance of party dictation, the man who is a fugitive in Canada for his
crimes against his country, the man who steals the
political power of a State, who bribes juries, falsifies
election returns, intimidates and counts out honest
voters, with all the negro-drivers and knights of the
lash and the shotgun, would not receive their usual
majorities for seats in Congress, or for the high judicial offices of the country.

Such non-partisan campaigns and elections are no
experiment in this and other civilized countries.
Partisan politics as an infection of the body politic is
a distemper of modern origin. It was many years
after the settlement of the country, and after we
became a nation, that political parties sprang into
existence and assumed anything like their present
authority over the destinies of the nation. The
fathers of the republic, who had earned their
liberties and prized them dearly, who were jealous
of any encroachment upon the sovereignty vested in
the commonwealth, were incapable of such conspiracies and usurpations of civil power. These
combinations were made possible by the stimulation
of foreign emigration and the consequent increase of
population, especially in towns and cities. The establishment of new industries, together with the
rapid accretion of wealth among the people, furnished resources for the spoils system, and made politics a more inviting field for the adventurer.

It is not by any means necessary, even when the people are deeply stirred to political action, that they should form a permanent organization and seek not only to carry into effect such reforms as they desire, but to hold indefinitely the powers and positions they have secured. We have had many examples in this country, during the last fifty years, where a great amount of honest political work has been done in seeking legislative action for the removal of great evils, without the formation of permanent parties. The friends of emancipation agitated the question and sought government action upon it for twenty years before they formed a third party in politics. The friends of temperance and those in favor of woman's suffrage have been in the non-partisan field seeking government action an equal length of time. These, with several other bodies and classes of citizens who have been engaged from time to time in canvassing public measures, inaugurating political campaigns, and carrying popular elections, have not found it necessary to employ the form of organization or tactics of the parties in order to move the public mind. Strange as it may seem, and quite inconsistent with all, it is the unanimous opinion of both Democrats and Republicans that it is the great mistake of their lives that the temperance men and the female suffragists have formed a third party. They very much fear it will prove their ruin. The sum of their testimony severally seems to be that distinct political organizations, after the pattern of the modern political parties, are not necessary as

agencies to instruct the public as to its political duties, or to awaken an interest that shall result in
salutary measures of reform.   They condemn their
own party associations when they advise a minority
of their fellow-citizens who are seeking justice
through State and national legislation to refrain
from party organization and not to make the principles and measures for which they contend political
issues.   It is a tacit admission that party organizations and party machinery are not needed to maintain a republican form of government, or to correct
abuses that may obtain under it.

I think there is discoverable a growing sentiment
to this effect among a large class of citizens.   When
distinct associations and movements for a reform in
political methods take a non-partisan phase; when
government officials and persons closely identified
with the existing parties find it almost impossible
longer to conduct certain branches of the public service through these coalitions; when it is a common
occurrence that special elections and elections to fill
the offices of the great municipalities are ordered
and successfully carried on the non-partisan basis;
when important questions of revenue and finance
have become so involved by party contention that
there is no hope of establishing any thing like a permanent policy in regard to them; when societies are
formed for the purpose of opposing or abolishing the
present parties as incompetent and corrupt, it is evi-
dent that a portion of the public, at least, are beginning to take a serious view of the subject which

has so long been treated with manifest indifference by the great mass of the voters of the country.

These organizations are of a century's growth in the very midst of us; fostered and defended by the people, they have assumed enormous proportions and begin to yield the ripened fruits that are the result of a generous culture. In some of the great municipalities, and in some of the more densely populated States, they seem to have reached a culminating point, or, at least, a crisis in their history of usurpation and misrule. In the city of New York, for example, it was found that the reign of law and order in some of the departments was practically suspended, that there was neither justice to be had in the courts, nor protection from fraud and violence to be obtained from the constituted guardians of the lives and property of the citizens. It was shown on investigation that the Police Department was a criminal conspiracy, of the boldest and most shameless character, a confederation of crime more dangerous and formidable than the aggregate criminality of the great metropolis. Chief of Police Byrnes, testifying before a committee of the New York State Senate, at the risk of admitting his own incompetency and criminality as a public officer, said, "The Department is honeycombed with abuses which have been growing for thirty years, and can be remedied only by radical legislation." Local politicians he claimed were the curse of the Department; and so long as politics were a factor in the Police Department, so long that state of things would exist. Although he had done his utmost to procure substantial information as to corruption and bribery, he was unable to get it; and the whole department was impregnated with the belief that protection had to be bought and that merit was of no avail.

The late W. H. Vanderbilt had previously expressed himself in language more terse and indignant in regard to the official profligacy existing in the city. He is reported to have said, "I live in a gang-governed, tax-ridden city, where the annual taxes are equivalent to paying rent. The real estate of this city is the property of the city officials, and the real owners are merely tenants. I can fight the wreckers in Wall Street more effectually than I can the thieves in the municipal government."

We see in New York, not only in the city, but in the State generally, the legitimate result of placing a great commonwealth, with its wealth, its commerce, and its populous cities, in the control of an irresponsible faction to rule its destiny. The friends of good government in the city had been laboring for years through the Republican and Democratic parties to correct the gross abuses of power and the profligate waste of the city's revenues, but without any appreciable success. They found it necessary to abandon existing political organizations and unite their efforts in a common non-partisan campaign of reform. On such a platform the present mayor of New York was elected. This gentleman and his friends have ever since his election been carrying on a somewhat vigorous contest with both the old parties; they seeking to regain their former ascendency, and he to administer the government of the city upon a non-partisan basis, in the interests of justice and the people and without party dictation or assistance. This non-partisan movement must in time extend throughout the State. The old parties will not submit to have the powers and emoluments of the city governments wrested from them, and they will continue a campaign of intrigue and intimidation to regain what they have lost, and retain their hold upon what is still in their grasp. This is destined to bring into the politics of the State a distinct non-partisan issue, an issue between the people and the parties, who shall rule the municipalities and the State. When that issue is distinctly made and is urged by a vigorous minority, I cannot doubt that the friends of honest government and clean politics will come to its aid.

The advocates of civil service reform must find sooner or later that they can make no term of compromise with the parties by which they will be deprived of the power they have so long enjoyed to control the offices of the State and collect and disburse its revenue; that no bipartisan schemes for joint occupancy or rotation in office will be satisfactory to either party in the controversy. Nothing but the destruction and repudiation of these organizations will restore the government of the commonwealth to the hands of the people or give any security to the State or to the nation.

There have been, furthermore, occasional utterances from men in public life and discussions of the

subject by the partisan press that encourage us to believe that there is an approaching crisis in the history
of the party organizations, when their incompetency
to deal with public questions, either intelligently or
impartially, will be clearly demonstrated to those
who now give them a loyal support.　During the discussions on the tariff in the Fifty-third Congress when
the Democratic and Republican parties were fiercely
contending on that question, and the passage of any
tariff measure seemed hopeless, a reporter of the New
York *Tribune* sought and obtained an interview with
Senator Manderson, of Nebraska.　The reporter pref-
aced the conference with the senator by saying,
"There are not a few members of both houses who believe that the tariff should be taken out of politics
almost entirely, and that it should be put into the
hands of business men and workingmen to settle in a
manner best to preserve and perpetuate the prosperity
of the nation."　The senator said, "There is a growing sentiment that some permanent disposition should
be made of the question, so that in the future changes
may be made in the tariff schedules without causing
such wide-spread disaster and distress.　It is the
opinion of many that the question, so far as practicable, should be taken out of the domain of politics,
and that in the future a commission be appointed from
among the very best men in the country to determine
any question that may arise with reference to customs
and protective duties."　The reporter adds, "This is
Mr. Manderson's belief in regard to the tariff.　It is

held by many members of Congress and it is a growing belief all over the country."

The partisan press sometimes gives utterance to such sentiments, moved to such discourse perhaps when an election has been defeated by party corruption or mismanagement, or when it has been found impossible to wrest a municipal government from the hands of a cabal of pothouse politicians who have driven it to the verge of bankruptcy. Here is an extract from an editorial of the New York *Tribune* which is quite in the line of the remarks just quoted of the senator from Nebraska. The *Tribune* says,—

"The desirability of removing the tariff question from the field of party politics is generally recognized, and numerous suggestions for the accomplishment of this end have been made. One of these suggestions has taken the form of 'A bill for the raising of revenue and creating a tariff commission and for other purposes,' which is to be submitted to Congress. Its author is Samuel B. Archer, of Newark, New Jersey, and for the promotion of the scheme a 'Tariff Commission League' has been formed, of which organization Mr. Archer is secretary and treasurer. The plan contemplates the establishment of a permanent tariff commission, non-partisan in its character, to be composed of one chief commissioner and eight associate commissioners, all of whom are to be appointed by the President, with the advice and consent of the Senate. It is proposed that this commission shall virtually have charge of all matters pertaining to the tariff, as the Interstate Commerce Commission has supervision over the commerce between the several States. The complete purification of municipal government will come only through the divorce of such government from partisan control."

Here is an extract from another partisan journal of similar import:

"These facts are rapidly becoming more and more apparent to the better class of citizens, and there is a rapidly growing tendency on the part of such citizens generally, without regard to party, to break away from party ties and act independently in purely local elections. This is an encouraging sign of the times, for it foreshadows the overthrow of boss rule, and of the intolerable domination of rings and cliques. It is an augury of wiser and more honest municipal government, in which the interests of party shall be subordinate to the interests of the people. It is an indication that the time is not hopelessly distant when city governments shall be conducted on business principles, and when the best men shall be selected as the heads of such governments, without reference to their political views."

I quote also an extract, entitled, "Machine Rule Waning," from the *Times* of our own city, a leading Republican journal of the State.

"The necessity for divorcing municipal governments from partisan control is becoming more and more apparent. The partisan machine is responsible for nine-tenths of the corruption and misgovernment which have disgraced so many of our cities, large and small, within the past generation. The case of Tammany is a conspicuous illustration. Tammany was simply a party machine brought to a high degree of perfection and kept in thorough working order by those who had it in charge. Had it not been for partisanism in municipal government the monstrous crimes of Tammany would have been impossible. The case of Tammany, though more conspicuous than others of its kind, is only one among many instances of the evil of too intense partisanism in municipal government. Men of progressive ideas are rapidly coming to recognize this evil, its source and its remedy. The trend of progress in better municipal government is distinctly away from partisanism and towards independence of action."

These journals, I believe, are both in favor of clean politics, and though they are heavily handicapped by their party alliances, they are working diligently and honestly to secure to the nation a purer and better service. I might here occupy many pages with extracts of this character from various partisan newspapers, but these are sufficient perhaps to indicate that the attention of the country is being called to the necessity of some radical organic change in the political situation.

The State platform of the Prohibition party of this State has this announcement:

"As it is a political impossibility to place the business interests of our country on a firm, reliable, and steady basis, while our tariff laws are subject to constant changes by the dominant parties, and while it is a subject of constant partisan dispute, we demand that the tariff question be taken out of the realm of party politics and be placed in the hands of a nonpartisan tariff commission where it can be regulated

14

to afford ample protection for the need of all industries and to provide sufficient revenue for the support
of the Federal government."

I have brought these several opinions together to
show that some, at least, of the leading minds occupied in public affairs are seriously considering the
question of non-partisan politics, a government by
the people, instead of the despotic rule of a joint
partnership of bosses and politicians. These opinions
are very significant, coming as they do from an intelligent partisan source. They are a confession of the
common fame charges brought by the people at
large against the current political conclaves that
their political system is a failure as an agency for
administering the government; that the time has arrived when other men and other measures must be
employed to save the nation from drifting into misrule and anarchy. It is a confession that Congress
has become incapacitated to legislate upon some of
the most important questions affecting the credit and
the general prosperity of the country. It is an admission that these parties can be dispensed with,
that the public have no proper use for their services.

If such difficult questions as the tariff and the
finances of the country can be settled and these
branches of the public service administered without
the aid of the party organizations, if it is better
policy to administer them on a non-partisan basis, if
non-partisan commissions will make better adminis-
trative officials than can be furnished us under party
rule, why not dispense with the parties and give us

the rule of men who neither wear a party collar nor make politics a trade?

It is comparatively of little consequence to us that the schools of philosophy, science, and religion, whom we permit to hold for us the keys of knowledge, may wrangle for centuries over questions in which we feel much interest, and make little or no progress in elucidating them. If they do not disturb the order and harmony of society, or retard its material prosperity, we do not lose confidence in their wisdom or their intentions. But when a great national body like the American Congress, to whom the people have committed the destinies of the nation, becomes so utterly demoralized and deadlocked by its factional strife for power and the spoils of office that its legislative functions are practically suspended, it is time that the causes, near or remote, which have given to the world a scandal so disgraceful and humiliating, should be unsparingly dealt with and speedily removed.

Unfortunately, those minor questions reckoned in the spheres of economics and political economy, which come nearest the daily life of every citizen and affect constantly the peace and comfort of every family in the land, are the problems most deeply involved and overslawed in the war of factions on the floor of Congress. Meantime, the hammer and the anvil, the saw and the plane, may be silent, the furnace fires go out, the wheels of commerce be retarded, and trade and agriculture languish, while the people wait and clamor for such legislative action as their necessities demand. Congress, debauched by party strife and ambition, refuses to suspend the intensity of the obdurate contest long enough to relieve the immediate necessities of the country. What wonder that there is a demand from many quarters that these questions be taken out of the political arena, as at present manned and equipped, and that there is a growing conviction of the incompetency of the great parties to rule the country.

The people must be blinded by party infatuation if they fail to see the dangerous tendency of this dispensation of spoliation and misrule. The country is weary of the domination of these combinations which destroy its peace and devour its substance without any adequate compensation for the injury. The public mind seems anxiously turning in all directions to find relief from their tyranny and exactions. The people are constantly calling for a change of administration; and it makes little difference which of the parties are in power, they fail to keep their pledges or to satisfy even those who most earnestly support them. What the people demand and seek is a change of morals and methods in the management of public affairs; this they hope to find in a change of parties, but are always disappointed. Attempts at reform have been made from time to time, some of them exceedingly vigorous, and which for a time promised permanent results, but they have proved thus far quite unavailing. The only visible purpose they seem to have served has been to bring charges of disloyalty and apostasy against the reformers and to deny them political fellowship or absolution. All attempts to reform an institution inherently and necessarily incompetent and corrupt must, of course, signally fail. It is like an effort to reform the drinking-saloon and the gambling-hell by "improving the services," instead of uprooting the business entirely.

It will be further objected to this radical method of renovating the public service and overthrowing party rule in the affairs of the nation that we have a system of civil service in operation under provisions of law, which is designed to correct these evils complained of.

While I am friendly to the system of civil service adopted by our government in the last few years, I do not share in the earnest expectations of that large class of patriotic and honest citizens who are seeking through this agency to purify the political atmosphere and give the country a non-partisan civil service. They may do much by classifying the clerical force of the government, establishing to some extent a merit system in appointments and promotions to improve the general efficiency of government employees; they may correct many of the grosser abuses that have arisen under the former promiscuous method of appointing persons to responsible positions under the government; but there can be no genuine reform, such as is demanded by the small minority who stand outside of political circles, while the great parties hold their present sway over the people. These organizations have been fed and nursed to their present large proportions upon the spoils of office. They depend upon government patronage for the sinews of war in their rival conflicts for the same prizes. The public offices and the emoluments and honors incident to the possession of them constitute their life blood. Without these resources they would have neither the means nor the incentive to sustain so vast an army in the active field against opposing forces; hence they will never consent to relinquish their hold upon these abundant and increasing resources of strength so long as they control, as they now do, the public press and a vast majority of the votes cast by the people. They may make concessions from time to time, as they are wont to do under the pressure of public indignation, but while the spoils of office are so necessary to their existence and while they continue to control the legislation, State and national, of the country, they will not relinquish their purpose to be fed and quartered at the public expense. As soon would an invading army surrender its provision train and its military chest.

What are the civil service advocates attempting to do? What is their wish and their hope? They want to eliminate from the civil service what is usually styled politics; they want to break up the system by which its patronage is controlled by politicians and parties, so that they shall no longer be the source of party spoils. A very worthy object. This means the destruction of parties. They cannot exist without supplies, and they have no other resource. A party without spoils or patronage must die for want of subsistence. I think for these reasons the great mass of the politicians and the partisan press are either secretly or openly hostile to the civil service law, and are determined to limit its operations to improvement of the general efficiency of the government employees.

The vote in the House of Representatives during a session of the Fifty-third Congress on the appropriation for the support of the Civil Service Department for the coming year was very significant of the prevailing sentiment in that body and among the people in regard to civil service reform. The vote stood 109 to 71 against the appropriation. Mr. Caruth, a member from Kentucky, expressed his satisfaction at the result of the vote by arising in his place and joyfully exclaiming, "If the old Democratic system of giving the offices to the victors was barbarous, then long live barbarism!" He undoubtedly voiced the general sentiment of his party on the subject. Some people prefer barbarism with the privilege of plunder to civilization with an honest occupation.

The chief purposes of the law are constantly obstructed if not practically nullified by both of the great parties which have been in power since its enactment. Very much the same routine of appointments and dismissals is in vogue as under the old system. With few exceptions, every man who has received an appointment under either administration has borne somewhere upon his organism the inevitable trademark of his party. The rule is to give patronage to the members of your own party when you can and to others when you must.

It is notorious that heads of departments and members of Congress are very ingenious and persistent in their devices to evade the spirit of the law. A favorite and very successful method for creating vacancies in the departments is to make an insufficient appropriation for the payment of salaries during the year; then at such a time as suits the convenience of the head of the department to do so, he gives notice to employees under him that as Congress has not appropriated sufficient money to carry them through the year, he shall be obliged to discharge a portion of the force. He proceeds under this decision to make vacancies in his department at his discretion; these are subsequently filled at the dictation of senators and representatives in Congress, who supply all this living material from their various constituencies.

The Congress is a sort of recruiting bureau for this service, and no man can be mustered into it who cannot be debited or charged to the patronage account of some member of Congress of the dominant party. It is a very easy matter to find very plausible pretexts for these changes in the various branches of the service on other ground than that of party preference. Men are discharged on the pretence of inefficiency and partisan activity. Old men who have been long in the service, who are experienced and valuable clerks of the department to which they belong, are discharged on the pretence that there is too much "dead wood" in the department; or on what is called the "economy dodge;" that is, by pushing work for a few months, perhaps by over-hours, everything in the bureau or division is up to date and work is slack, and then its chief finds that he can do with a lighter force, and discharges several of his men.

These devices and pretexts are quite a study with the appointing power of the government. Some men in government employ are regarded as experts in this kind of detective work. There was a chief clerk of the Treasury Department a few years ago, under the administration of Mr. Cleveland, by the name of Wiggins, who had a national reputation for his ingenuity in creating vacancies. He had the activity and scent of a sleuth hound in hunting out men that could be "bounced" on some plausible plea for their removal. It can never be reasonably expected that a partisan Congress will provide any legislation or authorize any rules under the Civil Service Commission that will deprive them of their hard-earned and long-established monoply of the government patronage.

"December 22. Representative DeForest, of Connecticut, chairman of the House Committee on Civil Service, to-day introduced a bill to exclude political influence in the appointment of postmasters. It provides that all postmasters now in office, or hereafter to be appointed, shall hold their offices during the session. The President is authorized to remove first-, second-, and third-class postmasters 'for cause communicated to the Senate' at the session following the removal. The Postmaster-General is also authorized to remove fourth-class postmasters 'for cause communicated in the letter of removal.'

"Section 3 provides that neither the President nor Postmaster-General shall appoint or remove a postmaster for political reasons upon political grounds, nor shall any post-office inspector recommend any person for appointment or removal on account of politics. The bill directs that the United States be divided into postal districts, each district to be presided over by a post-office inspector. When there is a fourth-class vacancy in the district the inspector publishes notices of the vacancy and issues blanks for applicants. The latter must show their capabilities of election, etc., for the place. No reference whatever is to be made of politics and no paper on politics is to be received. The inspector then makes a report to the Postmaster-General, and the appointment is made strictly on merit."

While it is not probable that any bill restraining the freedom of the appointing powers can pass either house, the bill here described never came to a vote. There is not a provision of it that cannot be evaded by the skill of the politicians. Such an act of Congress would prove a mere breastwork of straw against the attack of the horde of arrogant and cunning bosses of the great parties. All hopes of a better civil service founded on the reform of these organizations are in my opinion quite extravagant and futile. On the contrary, the spoilsmen are at present evidently getting impatient under the restraints of the civil service rules and enactments which lessen the opportunities of the place-brokers to ply their trade. The party revenues upon which their existence depends are endangered and naturally diminished. These efforts are apparent in several of the States and in the great municipalities of the country to rid themselves of this stumbling-block to party methods and general success. This is notably true in the State and city of New York, where the rule of the spoilsmen is almost supreme. They do not propose to repeal the present civil service legislation, but to attack the outworks of the system by supplying various amendments designed to destroy its efficiency, by diminishing the number of government employees who will be subject to examination under its rules.

When this reform was first introduced it struck the popular mind at once as a needed change. The politicians yielded to it as a necessary concession to public opinion. They did not comprehend at that time what they have since learned by experience, that the system has a direct tendency, and is at war with the efficiency and the very existence of the great parties by which the government is dominated. The bosses are now quite awake to the fact that they made a grave partisan blunder when they permitted legislation so disastrous to party rule and party discipline to become the law of the land. It does not require extraordinary sagacity to successfully predict the future course of the politicians of all parties in uniting to restore to these alliances all the power and patronage they formerly possessed. This they can do if they choose; and when they come to realize the facts of the situation they will be quite equal to it. It will not be long before there will be a union of these po-

litical parties to enter decisively upon this work. Mr.
Allen, senator from Nebraska, has very recently introduced a bill into the United States Senate to repeal
the civil service laws, and to do away with educa-
tional tests as preliminary to entering the public service. The new Secretary of Agriculture, Mr. Wil-
son, is, I see by Washington despatches, charged
with an open attack upon the civil service system.

The antagonism between the two forces is sharp and
well defined. The conflict is irrepressible, and the
spoilsmen must assert themselves in force or commit
hari-kari.

It is the misfortune of all great reforms that in
their early history they are hindered and delayed and
often ruined by a resort to temporary expedients to
diminish and modify the evil rather than to wholly
uproot and abolish it. The difference between these
two methods is the difference between success and
failure.

What is wanted in this emergency is a square issue
with these organizations and a life and death conflict
for their complete overthrow. Let the people resolve
that the parties must go, that their usefulness, if they
ever had any, has long since ceased, and that their
usurpations and spoliations shall have an end. The
people have long since raised the hue and cry against
them of stop thief! in every part of the land. Let
the friends of justice and honest politics join in the
pursuit and bring these artful dodgers to bay and to
final judgment for their crimes against civil liberty.
What is needed at this hour is a national non-partisan

movement for civil service reform, with a remedy sufficiently radical to reach the causes of the disease from which the body politic is suffering, the overthrow of the party oligarchies, and the restoration of the government of the country to the hands of the people from which it has so long been practically withheld.

There is in this country an increasing number of the earnest friends of good government, but they have no common aim to guide their exertions, no objective point to reach, save the modification of the present party system and the correction of the grosser abuses of the public service. Let this large and intelligent force of men and women who are in favor of clean politics and good government organize on a non-partisan basis, and they would cause their influence to be felt in every State of the Union. That such a movement is demanded, and that it would be responded to by a large number of citizens who are in earnest for some change in the administration of public affairs that a mere change of parties fails to bring, I cannot doubt. I believe the country would respond to such a timely and patriotic movement by giving it the support of thousands of men and women who are all ready for the work. They might with poetic justice, as well as good tactics, turn upon the parties the war-cry they have so successfully used in harassing and defeating one another,—"Turn the rascals out!"

www.ingramcontent.com/pod-product-compliance
Lightning Source LLC
Chambersburg PA
CBHW030323270326
41926CB00010B/1479